ULYSSES GRANT:

Personal Reflections

a novel

by

Victoria Sauers

Blue Bear Press

Pittsburgh, PA

Library of Congress Catalog Card Number: 98-93403

ISBN 0-966-62940-X

First Edition

Cover Photo: Ulysses Grant, 1880, used by permission of the Illinois State Historical Library

This book is dedicated to

Ulysses Grant and Sam,

with my thanks and appreciation for their courage

in telling their story

One evening, as I walked past the back room of my house, a room used only for storage, a shadowy figure caught my attention. He said his name was Sam and he asked that I write some things down for him, things "that need to be said." Unusual things started to happen--the light I leave on at night would be turned off in the middle of the night. I would smell cigar smoke in the house, although no-one smokes. The spirit of Ulysses Grant also appeared, stating that he had grown and changed, and that he wanted to tell "the rest of the story, the things that I left out in the past, and the things that I have learned since then."

The facts they gave were always accurate, things I had no way of knowing in advance, but always verified with research later on. The more I learned about Grant and about the events described in this book, the more I was impressed by his incredible courage and generosity of spirit in revealing this information so that others might learn these lessons too. The ghosts of Sam and Grant vanished shortly after they revealed the Epilogue on the way home from a research trip to the Military History Institute in Carlisle. Their work was complete, although

Sam has come back from time to time to make sure the material gets published.

For the sake of clarity, Grant in this story refers to Ulysses Grant, as he was in his lifetime. His helper spirit requested to be known as "Sam" and I am respecting that wish. The origins of Ulysses Grant's nickname, which is also Sam, is explored in the text contained herein. Sam and Grant are deeply intertwined, as we shall see, and this perhaps accounts for much of the enigma surrounding Grant.

This is their story.

Acknowledgements

In addition to thanking Ulysses Grant, Sam, and Julia Dent Grant, I would like to thank my father, Dr. Richard A. Sauers; Joe Dugan; Soldiers and Sailors Memorial Hall, Pittsburgh PA; Wendy Sauers; Carnegie Library of Pittsburgh; the Illinois State Historical Society Library; The Pennsylvania State University Library-McKeesport; and the U.S. Army Military History Institute. Thank you also to Randy McKenzie; you are a wonderful artist and friend. Thank you also to all my other friends; you know who you are. And a special thank you to my mom, for her encouragement and belief in my talent.

Disclaimer

This is a work of fiction. While many, many hours of historical research went into the preparation and writing of this book, it is nonetheless a novel. Neither the author nor Blue Bear Press shall have any liability or responsibility to any person or entity with respect to any loss or damage caused, or alleged to be caused, directly or indirectly, by anything contained within this book.

If you do not wish to be bound by the above, you may return this book in unused condition to the place of purchase for a refund consistent with their return policy.

ULYSSES GRANT:

Personal Reflections

March, 1998

New York

Chapter 1

A Sad Sack

Many of them looked like puffs of ether or clouds. Grant looked down. He supposed he looked like a puff too. "It has been so long, now," he thought.

He knew them all--their names, the litany of their complaints and their accusations against him. He had been far from blameless, he knew, in the misfortunes of all these people. When he was still alive yet, they had first come, in his dreams, in his tent on the battlefield at Shiloh. Piercing hideous screams of terror, in the dark of the night, when all should be silent.

His assistant, John Rawlins, had seen them too. Ah Rawlins, whose advice he had ignored. Rawlins, who had tried to bring some humanity to the whole war thing. The war had seemed like a chess game to Grant, the way they had taught it at West Point. "I need fifteen thousand troops," he had learned to say, as if he were ordering coffee. Now each one of those 15,000 came to him, wounded, crying out, accusing him. Their widows and their children cried out to him too.

"We were people, not troops," they said. "We were told this was for the good of our country. They never said we would die, that it would be mass suicide and not of our own choosing," they reproached him.

Rawlins himself reproached Grant. "I was your loyal assistant all those years, making sure you didn't get into trouble, seeing that you didn't drink, making you look good. And in return, you only mentioned me three times in your whole two volume <u>Memoirs</u>, with their 54 chapters about the Civil War."

Ah, Rawlins, sighed Grant. He had met the fiercely enthusiastic Rawlins in Galena, when Grant was working with his brother there. Rawlins was a Mexican War buff, and had been delighted to meet Captain Sam, as he was then known. They had spent many happy hours discussing the Mexican War. John Rawlins had been a lawyer, one of the ablest speakers in the state, and a candidate for elector on the Douglas ticket. Grant had offered him the position of Assistant Adjutant-General with the rank of Captain on his staff early in the War of the Rebellion, and Rawlins had accepted, despite being about to enter the service as the Major of a new regiment in the northwest part of Illinois.

Rawlins was right, thought Grant. He was always there for me, and I let him down by downplaying all the work he did during the Civil War when I wrote my memoirs. I could argue that I was a sick old man when I wrote them, but I knew what I was doing. I was in pain, but I had my full wits about me.

There was Charlie, one of the common soldiers, who had been killed in the battle of Cold Harbor. Charlie left behind his aged mother, his father having died in a farming accident two years earlier. She lost the family farm that had been in their family for over fifty years when no son returned home after the war to help take care of it. She died, penniless, in the Paupers Home in Chambersburg.

There were two old Army veterans, being driven from their homes in Paducah, complaining loudly.

There was Major Albertis, whose head had been shot off in the Mexican War, asking who would take care of his loved ones.

There was that meddlesome Captain Kountz, who used to interrupt the telegrams to General Halleck, causing all sorts of re-percussions.

There was even the ghost of his name, Hiram Ulysses Grant. When he had first gone to West Point, he had planned to register as Ulysses H. Grant, but his congressman had registered him as Ulysses S. Grant, using as his middle name Simpson, which was Grant's mother's maiden name. Grant had decided to change his name so that his initials would not spell the acronym HUG. On the trip to West Point he had felt much trepidation, and not only did he not want to be teased, he wouldn't have cared if he had never arrived at the school.

Grant looked around in the ether, discerning forms that were familiar to him. It had taken a while to get used to "seeing" things once he was no longer in physical form, but spirits could manifest as ether-y blobs or more like the forms they had had back on earth, which Grant preferred.

The sound of a horse brought to mind the horses Grant had known who had died. There was the one who had been shot out from under Hawkins during the battle at Monterey in the Mexican War. Its ghost whinnied reproachfully. And over there was another horse, the one that had been shot under Ulysses when they were moving upon Belmont in the War of the Rebellion. Even that horse Kangaroo that Grant had chosen on the return trip from Satartia, the one who was thusly named because he would rear up on his hind feet and make a plunging start whenever anyone got onto his back. Kangaroo reproached Grant for his use of spurs.

"I never knew animals had ghosts," thought Grant.

"And what about me," said his dog from back when Ulysses had been a boy. He had tried to reach out to pet him, but his hand had passed through the air.

Soldiers, both in blue and in gray. Tens of thousands had died in the War Between the States, and they blamed him. Soldiers from the Mexican War. Civilians.

Look, there was little Gregorio, the Mexican boy Ulysses had purchased during the Mexican War. He had brought him back with him to Detroit after the war, where

Ulysses was stationed and had a house with Julia, after Ulysses and Julia were married in August 1848. Gregorio was to serve as a valet and to attend their door and table. He left the Grants' service within a year, after some meddlesome neighbor had told Gregorio that he "could do much better for himself." He had been a nice cheerful boy, always willing to do whatever his master had asked, until that neighbor meddled, and then Gregorio had become sullen and withdrawn.

It never entered Grant's head at the time that buying a valet could be wrong. They were so cheap, and Julia's family had lots of these household helpers. And then there were the other things he had wanted Gregorio to do, but best to not think of such things, thought Grant, shaking his head.

Gregorio had said he was willing to stay until the Captain was satisfied for his passage from Mexico and his clothes and schooling. Captain Grant had said he was satisfied, and that Gregorio should just go. The boy had left, with a reproachful look in his eyes that had haunted Grant for years.

Grant looked off to the right, where the ghosts of a group of sailors were gathered. "Ah, the alleged mutineers on the *Suviah*," recollected Grant.

The ghost of one sailor floated over close to Grant. "You charged us with mutiny, and put us in irons. All because of the demented rantings of a man with consumption, our so-called captain."

"But I felt bad about it," protested Grant. "When you all submitted to being placed in irons without any resistance, I always doubted that you had mutinied. You all didn't seem to know about it until you were told."

"But you did nothing to stop him. He was crazy. You deprived us of our freedom," said the sailor.

"What could I have done?" said Grant. "Rules are rules. Can't have mutiny on a ship. I always felt bad I went back on board at that point and had to get involved. I'm glad the captain died before you all would have been tried."

"And we'd have hanged," said the sailor. "Some friend you turned out to be." He made a sound like harumph and disappeared into the ether with the masses of other ghosts.

Ghosts from the Mexican War, nameless soldiers, gaudily clad, with gaping wounds caused by muskets carried by the United States troops. And our soldiers too, reflected Grant, recognizing that brave artillery officer Major Ringgold, and Lieutenant Luther, also of the artillery. Enlisted men; officers. They had been counted separately in the battle reports, but here each soul was an equal.

Then there was Adam Badeau, thought Grant. He joined my staff in 1864 as aide-de-camp and military secretary. Seemed to be a fine fellow, and I kept him on through Reconstruction. He helped me write <u>Military History of Ulysses S. Grant, Vol. 1</u>, which we published in 1868, and then I sent him to the consulate in London the following year, where he was to continue to work on the subsequent volumes.

Took him years, reflected Grant. I don't think we saw Volume 2 until 1881. Then he wrote that nice book <u>Grant in Peace</u>. Used to make me feel so good. Grant sighed. Until I hired him to assist with writing my memoirs, once I realized I was dying and Julia would need the money the memoirs could bring in order to support herself.

Yes, reflected Grant, that's when the trouble with Badeau started. I offered to pay him $5,000 from the first $20,000 the book cleared in profits, and $5,000 from the next $10,000. But it apparently wasn't enough for him, although it seems like a huge sum of money to me. He'd have been set for life. Then he got greedy after he moved into my house. Said he wanted $1,000 a month and $20,000 on top of that. So Fred and I decided we had had enough, and put him and his extortion scheme out of the house. I did the rest of the work myself, with my son Fred helping me check the facts.

"You owe me $10,000 under the original agreement," came Badeau's voice into Grant's brain.

"You didn't do anything to earn the money," replied Grant. "You got greedy, and wanted to steal more money from me, a sick old man, and from the profits my poor widow would need in order to subsist. You were scum."

"And you were unfair. I was a loyal servant to you all those years, writing your books, keeping your notes," said Badeau. "And this is the thanks I get? HUNH!" The ghost snorted in disgust and floated off.

Even those two young Union soldiers who had gone off on their own at Salt River, Missouri, to look for rebels. They had left in the afternoon after the tents were pitched, stayed out all night, and returned with a "secesher" and two of his horses the next day. Grant did not rise from his seat of pull the pipe from his mouth as he asked, "Who gave you permission to be absent from camp?"

Grant had had the two boys tied to a tree for six hours as punishment, until that Reverend James Crane had persuaded him that the punishment did not fit the crime, that it was far too harsh for two enthusiastic young boys who thought they were helping the Union cause. Grant had then released the boys, and sent the "secesher" home.

Grant sighed. The ghosts, he thought, I can see them all--men, women, children; soldiers, civilians; places--battlefields, houses, palaces, cabins; and a chair.

A chair? I must be losing my mind, to worry about a chair, reflected Grant.

"Yes, a chair," came a thought into his mind, confirming what he himself had been thinking.

"You think a chair is important?" Grant asked this new spirit.

"As a matter of fact, yes," said the spirit, giving nothing away.

"What kind of chair?" mused Grant. There had been simple ones in his boyhood home, that his mother

Hannah Simpson Grant had chosen, austere chairs that reflected her no-nonsense personality. Then there were those uncomfortable chairs without backs in school, to enforce good posture. Must not have worked, thought Grant. My posture was poor up until West Point, and even then I barely squeaked by in the posture department.

Hmmm, mused Grant, pondering the issue of chairs. There were those two glorious mahogany chairs I had made to go with our first dining room table, back when Julia and I were first married. Grant sighed. Julia's feet had been a full twelve inches off the ground when she sat in one of those chairs, but he had solved that problem by having a matching set of little footstools made to match the two big chairs. And dear Julia had never complained, just laughed in that silvery little laugh of hers.

That I had been able to fix, reflected Grant, but these ghosts, I don't know how to fix them. A wave of despair swept over him, and Ulysses felt as if he were weeping.

Dear God in Heaven, I need peace. It is time to rest. I cannot suffer this way anymore. I am a broken man. I have wronged so many people. I want to change, to grow, and to find peace. I don't know where I am right now; this place is certainly not heaven. Maybe it's hell. Maybe it's purgatory. I don't know. All I know is that for over a hundred years now, I've never had more than an hour's respite from this suffering. Dear God, please help me. In the name of Jesus and any of the saints, who I can't remember, please, please help me.

Chapter 2

Sam

"Who are you?" asked Grant. This new oval-shaped puff seemed familiar, and not as menacing as the others. Grant noticed a light and a warmth coming from this spirit. In fact, he seemed, well, kind.

I am kind, came the thoughts, directly into Grant's brain as if the words were placed there. That's how it always was, since he had died, Grant reflected. He didn't need to use his ears to hear; the words just came into his brain, if indeed it was still a brain that he had.

I am Sam, and I am your guardian spirit, the part

of you that works for the greater good. Sam did his best to manifest in as close to a human form as possible, so that Ulysses would feel comfortable.

Ulysses, too, manifested as close to his old human form as he could, to dialogue more properly with this new person.

"Can you help me? Please tell me it is not impossible. I can't take the suffering anymore," said Grant.

Sam looked at Grant, at his big blue eyes, so incredibly full of sorrow and pain. He knew at once that Grant did not exaggerate the depth of his suffering. Of all things, the eyes never lied. In fact, people's eyes usually looked the same in each of their lifetimes.

"Tell me a little more about what's bothering you," suggested Sam.

Grant nodded. "That should be easy. There are so many things. I guess the toughest part is in figuring out where to begin."

"The journey of a thousand miles starts with but a single step," said Sam. "To quote a famous philosopher."

Grant thought, and from the wretched depths of his despair, the words poured out in torrents. "I have done wrong by so many people. I never planned for my life to turn out this way. I feel so bad. The ghosts, they crowd around me, day and night, unceasing, moaning, crying, reproaching me. There are ghosts from both of the wars I served in, Mexico and the War of the Rebellion. Soldiers from my side, soldiers from the other side. They blame me for their deaths. Young ones. Old men being turned out of their houses. People I worked with, people I trusted, like Adam Badeau, who was to help me write my memoirs. Household servants, slaves. Horses. Even a chair. I am a haunted man. I have no rest. The noise never stops. My life on earth was one of despair and bleakness. Everyone saw me as a hero, but no one ever bothered to find out about the real me. I am trapped, and alone, and miserable. I would wish I was dead, but I already am. Now I just want peace."

Sam admired Grant's honesty. Much of what Grant had just said was already known to Sam, for Sam had been assigned to help Ulysses way back in 1839, when Ulysses had set out for West Point at his father's insistence. Young Hiram Ulysses Grant's spirit had called out for help, and the spirit Sam had answered him. Of course, reflected Sam, Ulyss hadn't listened very well when he was alive, but now he was paying rapt attention to the spirit who had been his guardian angel for a hundred and fifty-nine years now.

"From your lowest point," said Sam, "you are now ready to rise up, for there is no other direction to go."

"So what do we do now?" asked Grant. "Give me a list, tell me what to do, and I shall do it. Anything you say, anything to relieve this horrible suffering."

"There is a long list of things you must review and learn," replied Sam. "Some are things you learned many years ago at your mother's knee but forgot, things you heard in church but decided didn't apply to you, times your ambition or that of those around you blocked your understanding, or your cowardice interfered, and you said nothing to stop that which you knew was wrong."

"So much wrong," despaired Grant in an anguished tone. "How can I ever begin to make amends? There must be thousands of these spirits who blame me for their difficulties."

"It cannot be done all at once. Your life lasted for sixty-three years, and you have been here in the ether now for a hundred and thirteen years," answered Sam.

"Wow, you have a clear sense of time," said Grant

with admiration.

"And you will too, when you have sorted all this out," said Sam. "A person can't do the work of sorting this all out by him or herself. They need a helper. I am your helper. I first came to you long ago, back in 1839 when you were heading for West Point, but you didn't listen to my suggestions. I've been here in the background of your existence ever since, checking in on you periodically, and it's always been the same. I would make suggestions, but you just weren't ready to hear them. I commend you for finally realizing you need help to sort this out."

"Then there's hope for me?" asked Grant, scarcely wishing to hope.

"Yes, there is hope. No matter how vast a person's sins are, God's love is so great that He will never forsake you. You just have to find the way home to Him again, and the way will be provided for you. Not that it will be easy," cautioned Sam.

"No, but whatever it takes, I will do it. I will work so hard, you will be proud of me," promised Grant.

"The list is long, and so as to not frighten you, I will ask that you trust me, and we will go one item at a time. There are fourteen items we must go over, and I will reveal them to you one at a time. For now, the important thing is that you have accepted my help. That alone is a tremendous accomplishment, and I am proud of you for being ready to take this step."

Grant nodded. "Anything, so long as this suffering will end. I am so wretchedly unhappy, with no rest and no hope for any. Please help me. I will do as you say. Help me find the way home." His eyes were filled with unshed tears.

"In the manner of Homer's Ulysses, this will be an epic journey. Just as the metalworker passes steel through the flames to strengthen it, so too will you be strengthened. Just remember, the longest journey begins with but a single step. I will be with you on this journey, every step of the way," said Sam.

"Thank you. Just knowing that you are here helps," said Grant, feeling himself growing sleepy, warm and comforted, like a ship coming into its harbor.

Ulysses felt his eyes closing, and he rested for two hours, more than he ever had since he had died, back in 1885.

Chapter 3

The Golden Rule

Grant awoke then, eager for his teacher to begin the lessons that would lift him out of this morass he had wallowed in for so many years. "Where is he?" wondered Grant, when Sam did not immediately appear.

"Patience," said Sam, when he finally did appear some time later. The warmth and light that accompanied Sam gave some comfort to Grant. "I have other people to help too."

"Oh," said Grant. "I hadn't considered that."

Grant was silent for a few moments. Finally he

spoke again, when Sam did not immediately volunteer information. "So what's today's lesson?"

"It's an easy one," said Sam. "What is the Golden Rule?"

"Damn, my brain must be getting really fallow," said Grant, trying to think of the Golden Rule. "It's something simple, I know. I can remember my mother teaching it to me when I was little. The teachers used to say it too, especially in the early grades." Grant struggled to remember.

"Aha!" said Grant. "Hon y soit qui mal y pense."

"Interesting choice," remarked Sam. "That one says 'Evil things to those who think evil thoughts.' It's true of course, but is focused on evil and bad, rather than focusing on the good and heading toward the light, shall we say. It's another way of saying we reap what we sow."

"Then I'm doomed," said Grant. "I can't even remember the Golden Rule."

"You're not doomed," said Sam. "Remember, I'm helping you. Once you admit you can't do it without God, He reaches down a big hand to help you pull yourself up. Now try again to see if you can think of the Golden Rule."

"Do no harm," suggested Grant.

Sam nodded. "That's a good one, the one we teach the physicians. You're getting closer. It has to do with a fundamental truth of the universe."

"There's nothing certain in life but death and taxes," offered Grant.

Sam shook his head, although Grant could sense a hint of amusement in the spirit, his angel he supposed.

Suddenly, Grant heard his mother's words come into his brain, or his consciousness, as Sam told him it was called. "Do unto others as you would have them do unto you," repeated Grant, just as he heard it.

"Good," said Sam. "Now let's see how that applies in your life. Who said the following quote? 'The art of war is simple enough. Find out where your enemy is, get at him as soon as you can, strike him as hard as you can and as often as you can, and keep moving on.' Now who said that?"

Grant thought. "It's a really good quote. It works, too. Hmmm, and it sounds familiar. Alexander the Great, maybe?"

Sam's eyes twinkled. "I doubt it," he said. "Maybe back when he was a fierce warrior and conqueror, but not once he became a man of peace, working for God."

"Wasn't he Macedonian? Didn't he believe in the Greek gods?" asked Grant, momentarily relieved from finding an answer to yet another difficult question.

"Yes, he was Macedonian, and in that lifetime he did believe in the Greek gods. However, we all continue to grow and develop, whether we are in human form or here in spirit form. And one of the highest truths we learn is that there is One God, and that all other manifestations of God, such as the Greek gods, and the prophets and such, are all from God, as a way to bring the message to human beings in a way that the humans can understand. When God speaks directly to people, the vast majority of people don't seem to listen very well. In fact, in modern day down on earth, if a person admits to hearing God's voice, the doctors say that the person is psychotic and they medicate the person or lock them up, to take away the voices."

"Incredible," said Grant. "And sad, too. I would have loved for God to speak directly to me."

"Would you have listened to Him?" asked Sam, mildly amused.

"Probably not," replied Grant, with his usual honesty. "But it would have been flattering to know that he cared that much about me that he tried to talk to me."

"He does care about you and for you," replied Sam. "That's why He sent me to help you. God can't always be everywhere at the same time, so He has a lot of us spirit helpers, or angels, to use the more popular term, helping Him. It's good practice for us, too, because in order to help someone, we have to be really sure of God's teachings. Then, when we've proven that we can walk as close to His path as possible, we get to move on to the next plane."

"So we're not stuck here, in whatever this place is, forever?" asked Grant.

"No, not forever," said Sam. "But each person or spirit, since that's the part that survives with or without a physical body, grows at his or her own pace. We can't force someone to learn more rapidly. All we can do is to present the lessons and let the person do the studying themselves. There are no tests, per se. You and God will know when you've learned the lessons adequately. I'm your personal tutor, so to speak. So anyhow, who said that last quote about war?"

Grant thought a moment, stroking his beard. "Hmm," he said. "I think it was myself who said it."

"And what kind of effects would such a strategy have, besides the one you're thinking of, which is to win a war. Are there any other effects to striking as hard as you can and as often as you can?" said Sam.

Grant thought and replied, "Nope, it's a sound theory."

"Let's try an analogy," suggested Sam. "If a parent were to behave that way, would that be a kind parent or a mean parent?"

A light went on in Grant's head. "Oh! It hurts people. Is that why all the ghosts came? I messed up their lives, and now they do the same to me?"

"In a manner of speaking," said Sam. "We do reap that which we sow, and when we harm others or fail to do the 'right' thing, it comes back on us, not to be malicious necessarily, but so that we can learn from it. Some people just have to be hit harder with the message before they figure things out, to use your own choice of words."

"I must be pretty dense if I need thousands of ghosts to tell me the message," said Grant, ruefully.

"The point is that you did figure it out. Now I want you to figure out how to work the Golden Rule for the Greater Good of humanity. Think about it and when I come back, we'll discuss it."

"Good," thought Grant. "Tactics. I can do this."

"Yes, you can," said Sam. "Just don't get cocky. Remember, a person has to learn to crawl before he can walk." And with that, Sam disappeared into the rest of the ether.

After Sam left, Grant spent a lot of time thinking. Do unto others as you would have them do unto you. Apparently, I've done wrong unto thousands of people. Now how do I reverse this? Seems it should be easy. If these ghosts were the enemy, I could encircle them and starve them out; I could drop a bomb on them, or shoot them. I could demand that they surrender.

Wait, thought Grant, Sam would say that was doing more wrong again. Maybe I have to do something nice for each of them. No, that would take thousands of years, though, and I don't think Sam means for me to suffer that long. It's kind of nice to know that he's been there, watching me, since right before I started West Point.

And here I thought the other Animals as we were called in our first year came up with my nickname after I had been registered as Ulysses S. Grant, instead of the Ulysses H. Grant that I was going to use. Oh well, can't help the fact that my mother's maiden name was Simpson, and that's what the governor put as my middle name. Then instead of my initials being HUG, they were U.S. Grant, U.S. as in United States, so they started calling me Uncle Sam, and then later Captain Sam, when I was in the Mexican War.

Isn't it interesting that my spirit helper's name is Sam too? Maybe the name thing was no coincidence. Maybe Sam was the part of me that still knew right from wrong, that knew that it would be better for me to get lost en route to West Point, back when I prayed the barge would capsize.

The part of me that wanted to quit the Army and be a mathematics professor at a college in Ohio. The part of me that wanted to be a farmer, or to work with horses. The part of me that sat on the cliff near West Point, the gentle dreamer.

The part of me that knew that war was wrong, that I shouldn't be a part of it. To think he was there all along, and I didn't know it, or if I did, I didn't listen to him. Grant sighed.

Well, I better get back to the assignment. Sam said there was a whole list of things to cover, and this is just the first assignment. Although it might get easier once I get the hang of this.

An image of a chair popped into his head, a wooden chair, some kind of dark wood, with a reclining back.

Maybe I'm supposed to sit in the chair to think. Grant considered this idea. Well, I'm a puff of air type thing, so I guess I just have to think of myself sitting in the chair.

He pictured himself sitting in the chair, and found himself exactly there, in the chair. Wonder if it'll help me with the assignment? Grant pondered this, stretching out by reflex into the reclining pose he had always favored.

Now, if I had some thing to smoke, he thought. I always think better with something to smoke.

A skinny ghost of an old man floated by, coughing as he went. "Smoking causes cancer. I died of cancer of the lung. You died of cancer of the throat. Give it a rest," he said as he floated past Grant. Grant remembered him; he had met the man in the waiting room of that doctor's office, the special doctor that Julia had found for him, to see what could be done about the cancer and that awful pain.

Grant smiled to himself and shook his head ruefully. "Nothing to smoke, then. Now let's see."

The assignment proved tougher than it looked and the next time Sam appeared, Grant had to confess that he hadn't thought of anything yet, since the scope of the problem was so vast.

"So what have you figured out so far?" asked Sam the next time he came to see Grant.

"Well, I'd have to do nice things for thousands of people and that will take many, many years. Do you really want me to continue suffering that long?" asked Grant.

Sam chuckled. "There's no easy answer. All those lives that you affected--the soldiers, their families, their offspring that were left without a father, the future generations that never occurred--this is not a simple matter."

"No, sir, I see that," said Grant, lapsing into the military style of speaking that had been drilled into his head at West Point.

"No need to be formal," said Sam. "I'm your

helper, remember; I'm here for you. So let's think about what you can do to show you know the Golden Rule."

Grant thought a moment. "I guess I could make a vow from this point forward that I will always consider all the possible consequences of my actions and never intentionally do anything that will harm anyone else."

Sam nodded. "That's a great idea. You can't go backward, but you can change from this point forward. That's a good start. How will you know if something could harm someone?"

Grant considered this, stroking at the beard that was no longer visible on his face. "Well, anything that kills someone wouldn't be too good. Anything that wrongfully deprives someone of their money wouldn't be too good. I know how upset I was when I lent that Hunt character from the Fourth Infantry several hundred dollars to start a business, and then when I needed the money back, he was nowhere to be seen. Couldn't find him out West, nor back in Sackett's Harbor."

Sam listened patiently. "Go on."

"Never to betray the trust of anyone who believes in me; to not go to dance halls alone or out drinking when I should be at home with my wife and children. I did Julia many terrible wrongs by going out and gambling away our money and drinking, and she only ever reproached me once. That's when I took the Temperance pledge," said Grant.

"Ah yes," sighed Sam, "the Temperance pledge. Lasted what, a few weeks, until you went to Vancouver and saw your old buddy Rufe Ingalls, who told you it was so boring out there that there was nothing to do but drink. Oh, and then you got the letter from Julia telling you that your second child was a son and that she had named him Ulysses S. Grant, Jr. So you had 'four-fingers of whiskey' to celebrate, and before you knew it, you were drinking more than ever."

"But it _was_ boring out there," said Grant.

"That's no excuse for drinking," said Sam. "Boring means you needed to read or find interesting educated people to learn from. Had you saved all your money, you would not have returned home from California in debt, penniless and reeking of vomit and alcohol."

"I know," said Grant. "I am deeply ashamed of that behavior."

"You even told Julia that she couldn't come with you to the West, although she cried and begged to come with you. You claimed that the passage there would be rough and that you didn't earn enough to support her and your children," said Sam.

"The passage was rough. One out of every seven passengers died en route," said Grant, in his own defense.

"But what about the money issue? You were in charge of the division of married soldiers with their families, and lots of the privates as well as officers managed to support their families on a soldier's pay. Housing was provided and they got to buy provisions at government wholesale rates. You could have done it, but you didn't want to," commented Sam.

"But Julia was used to a fancy life, with servants and crystal and parties and cotillions," said Grant.

"Pshaw," said Sam. "You didn't even think of Julia, at least not as a primary consideration. You did what you wanted to do, and we won't even get into a discussion of that little blond-haired wife of that one first lieutenant, and how she factored into your decision to leave Julia home."

"But that was just physical," said Grant.

"We'll discuss that issue later," said Sam. "For now, you need to stay focused on the Golden Rule and how you can demonstrate that you have learned it."

Grant sighed. "I've made so many mistakes," he said.

"Let's re-frame that," said Sam. "You've made lots of opportunities for your own growth and development. You've found out a lot about yourself, in terms of what not to do, what didn't bring you peace and happiness. For instance, if I were you, I would never ever touch alcohol or any form of psychoactive drug again, in any lifetime."

"But all the officers drank. It's part of the lifestyle," said Grant.

"So you didn't need to be an officer then," said Sam. "There are always choices. We might not like those choices because our vision gets clouded by other people's expectations, like your father's plans for you as his son. And we'll learn more about that as we go on. But personally, Ulysses, between you and me, I don't think anyone should drink. The body is the temple of the Lord and should be treated with respect. It's the vessel that carries your spirit while you're on earth learning valuable lessons. It's a trusty friend that accompanies you through one lifetime, and then it returns to dust, and you get a new one.

I've seen so many people make mistakes because of alcohol; between wasting money, and losing time that could have been spent learning things and working on improving one's relationships with others, to jobs that have been lost because of poor performance from the effects of the alcohol, like the job you lost out West. People have had affairs while drinking, have yelled at their bosses and coworkers and family and friends. People on alcohol have had bad accidents where others are killed. Alcohol has destroyed whole civilizations. It's one of the worst things the white man ever gave to the Indians." Sam took a breather. "All in all, I don't think people should drink."

"But it's an escape," said Grant.

"And if you need an escape, you are certainly smart enough to find one that doesn't involve alcohol," said Sam. "Which brings us back once again to the Golden Rule, Grant. You keep avoiding the issue."

Grant sighed. "I guess I could go back to some of the people I wronged and do nice things instead. Or I could do nice things for strangers."

"Atta boy, Grant, I knew you'd think of something. How about you practice random acts of kindness, and do something nice for someone who doesn't expect it, like preventing a little old lady from tripping down her steps, or stopping a mugging? You're a spirit now, and we're called angels when we do things like this. For many, such as yourself, it's a part of rehabilitation and therapy. The world contains a lot of people who have been cruel and need to make it up by kindness now. So, in addition to the random acts of kindness, I'd also like you to follow up on some of the descendants of people like John Rawlins and Gregorio, and do something nice for them too."

Grant nodded. "I can do this. And this will erase the wrongs I've done?"

Sam shook his head. "No, it won't erase them, unfortunately. What's done is done. This is more like rewriting a term paper. The first draft is still there, but people look at the most current edition. So we can always improve ourselves. If we do good, then good will come our way too, expanding that which is good in the universe."

"What if I see bad things going on in the world?" asked Grant.

"That's a very good question, Ulys. I remember

years ago when you said 'Experience proves that the man who obstructs a war in which his nation is engaged, no matter whether right or wrong, occupies no enviable place in life or history. Better for him, individually, to advocate 'war, pestilence, and famine' than to act as obstructionist to a war already begun'."

"I remember that," said Grant.

"We all have a choice to do good or to do evil in life," said Sam. "Sometimes we think we're doing good, like being a good commander in war, but it's actually something bad, because it kills millions of God's creations. We have to weigh all the factors, and think about things from the perspective of God and of the Greatest Good. And sometimes that means stopping people who are on a bad path. For instance, if someone had stopped Hitler in the 1930s, millions of lives would have been spared. Sometimes it's better to stop one person than allow many to suffer."

"So you're saying someone should have killed Hitler," said Grant. "I thought you said that killing is wrong."

"Killing is wrong," said Sam. "I didn't say to kill him, I said he needed to be stopped. You can capture someone and lock them up or move them to stop them. When someone harms others, they need to answer for that, whether in the current lifetime or after they die. And then they have to make amends. It's that simple. Think of it as cause and effect. You always have to pay the piper, to go back to a long-ago analogy."

Grant considered this message and nodded. "Thanks Sam," said Grant. "Now I need to get busy."

"Bye, Grant, I'll see you in awhile," answered Sam as he disappeared. And the light faded, as it always did.

Chapter 4

No Other Gods Before Me

Grant was eagerly looking forward to today's lesson with Sam, for each day would bring him closer to his goal of finding peace within himself, of helping his restless spirit to settle down.

Sam arrived in his customary burst of light, and Grant greeted him with enthusiasm. "I'm glad to see you so enthused," said Sam. "Not many of my students have been as dedicated," he said.

"When I make up my mind to do something, I stay on that path until it's accomplished," said Grant.

"And that determination can work for or against you, looking over the course of your life. But here, it will work for you, by helping you master the lessons you need to review or to learn, and then to help you put things together to find your own answers, to guide yourself in future," said Sam.

"So what are we discussing today?" asked Grant, staying on target, goal-oriented as usual.

"We'll be discussing the ten commandments," said Sam.

Grant smiled. "So the next ten lessons are those commandments."

"Right," said Sam. "The ten commandments come from God; He first gave them to Moses when the Jews were in the desert after they were led out of slavery, and the people were really struggling. Many were unclear about God and His message, and lived in unhealthy ways, stealing and lying and committing adultery and murder. Moses himself had even killed someone. So God spoke to Moses, who had the good sense to listen to the Lord and to write down the guidelines for living that God wished His children to live by. They are an excellent set of guidelines to help people walk as close to the path of <u>God</u> as possible.

And I personally think it was positively inspired of God, if I'm not being presumptuous, to make it ten commandments, since humans have ten fingers, so that they could remember the commandments by reciting them as they touched each finger. Memory helps such as this are excellent with people who can't read or write, and people who like the reassurance of having a concept turned into something they can touch or feel or count."

"So did the people follow God's commandments?" asked Grant, with curiosity. "From a military point of view, one would expect that orders coming down from on high would most certainly be obeyed."

"True, that is the military perspective," said Sam, "And one with which I myself am well-acquainted also. But, to answer your question, the people tried to follow the commandments, but it is always a struggle, through each successive lifetime, until the person realizes that the true path to peace and tranquility is to walk as close to the path of God as possible, and to stop focusing on what the person feels like doing if it is something that goes against God's teachings."

"But don't I get to choose what I want to do in my lifetime?" asked Grant, perplexed.

"Sure," replied Sam. "You can choose where and when and to whom you will be born. You can choose your occupation unless you've chosen parents who will push you into a particular occupation. You can generally choose your spouse, unless you are born into a society where children are betrothed by their parents in arranged marriages."

"Why would someone choose to do that?" asked Grant.

"There are lots of reasons. Maybe to learn to trust that the universe will provide the lesson they need to learn. Maybe to see what it's like to have a major decision made for you by your parents. Maybe to work out issues with your parents. Maybe to punish oneself for making bad choices in a previous lifetime. Maybe to avoid making choices. There are many, many reasons. But to get back to the commandments, let's look at adultery for instance."

"Adultery?" asked Grant.

"Yes, being unfaithful to one's spouse, which I will define as including flirting with others, as well as the more usual definitions. Anyhow, God specifically prohibits adultery, in two different commandments, which we'll discuss more later. So, while you can choose to get married, and choose your spouse, you also have to choose to honor the wedding vows to love, honor and obey, and honor means to be faithful to. Nonetheless, many, many people break this vow and commandment. What effect would that have on the marriage?" asked Sam.

Grant considered this a moment, thinking about his own experiences and that of his male friends. "I guess if the other person didn't know, it wouldn't hurt them," he said.

"Do you really think the spouse doesn't know?" asked Sam.

Grant nodded.

"People often believe what they want to believe," acknowledged Sam. "But the person who breaks one of God's commandments knows that what he or she did was wrong, and must live with that knowledge of wrong-doing. I would say guilt, but only some of the perpetrators of this injustice feel guilt. Some seem to think it's their right to do whatever they want, without any thought for the consequences. And when God made humans, He gave them the freedom to make choices, be they right or wrong choices. But as I've already said, choices..."

"...Come with consequences," Grant said, finishing Sam's sentence with a smile.

"Right," said Sam, nodding in approval. "So yes, people can do whatever they want, but they need to think of the consequences. Is it worth hurting one's spouse or one's children? Lots of times, the children suffer just as much when a parent is unfaithful, because the children know that the parent's energy is attached elsewhere, not within their family. That's a difficult burden for children to carry. Many children of parents who were unfaithful have trouble ever marrying or having a faithful marriage. So the closer we follow God's commandments, the easier it is for our children."

"I can see that," said Grant, a far-off look in his eyes.

"Now we need to consider the first commandment and what it means," said Sam. "Thou shalt have no other Gods before me."

"You mean like the Greek gods?" asked Grant.

"I believe God means that He is the One True God. God created everything in the universe, and that would include the Greek gods, and the Roman gods, and any other messengers of the word that one can think of. But humans often worship 'false gods' such as power or

money or fame. When those things become more important than following God's word, then they have become a
'false god,' because they receive the energy and effort that
should go to God instead."

"Is that where the phrase about how it is easier for
a camel to pass through the eye of a needle than for a rich
man to get to heaven comes from?" asked Grant.

"Probably so," said Sam. "People get caught up
in power games. They want to have power over other
humans, and they forget that to God alone belongs dominion. We are all children of the same God, and so no one
human is greater than any other. But lots of people don't
want to see it that way. There are whole hierarchies in the
business community that are based on power and money,
with the person with the most power or money being
revered as one would revere a god. So power and money
are false gods."

Grant nodded, thoughtfully.

"Then there is the military hierarchy," said Sam.
"Military people follow a chain of command, and in order
for the system to work, people have to do what their
superior says. They put their faith in a human being, and
human beings are fallible. The goal in war is 'winning',

by which one side achieves power over another side. Sometimes they gain land or money or material resources. There is more than enough land and resource for everyone on the earth, if we use our resources wisely. However, not only is 'winning' a false god, military people make many sacrifices to this false god. They sacrifice their integrity and they sacrifice human blood to this false god of 'winning'."

"It sounds so barbaric, put that way," said Grant.

"You're right. War _is_ barbaric. And unnecessary."

"Unnecessary?" asked Grant. "But we have to defend the unity of the nation, and to stop oppressors and the like."

"Sure, we need to stop oppressors, but we can put them in jail, and not necessarily kill them. We can fight our battles on paper only, and not involve human lives. Fighting for a principle sounds great, but the loss of human lives is a far greater loss than any principle humans are usually fighting about."

"But we couldn't just let the South secede," said Grant. "Although I am tempted to think that if the men who wrote the Constitution had realized that someday brother would fight against brother over the slavery issue and the issue of keeping the United States together, then they would have included a provision to allow a dissenting state to leave the Union, rather than there be bloodshed."

"So you can see both sides of this issue," said Sam. "There was the lofty principle of keeping the country intact, versus the loss of life that comes with war. And the boundaries were very blurry for the War of the Rebellion. You and your wife owned slaves, and yet you were a Union general. Generals on both sides of the war were men you had gone to school with at West Point. So you both had the capability of winning, and you'd all studied the same lessons. What was really the point? Would your life have been that different if the South had seceded, if it had simply been allowed to occur?"

"I guess it would depend on whether we were living in Galena, Illinois, or St. Louis, Missouri. Illinois, we wouldn't have had any slaves. We'd have had to leave them behind with friends or relatives in the South. In Missouri, we'd probably have had Colonel Dent's planta-tion, and it would have thrived on slave labor."

"Which brings up other issues," commented Sam. "But we'll talk more about slavery later. So, in a way, maintaining the Union became a false god, one that people made human sacrifices to, killing in order to keep it going."

Grant thought about this a moment, as a vision of a large volcano and a primitive tribe popped into his head. The same image appeared in Sam's head at the same time.

"Sort of like primitive people who sacrificed to the volcano god so the volcano wouldn't explode," said Grant. "The volcano would erupt irregardless, but it made the people feel better, and gave them a feeling of control over their situation. But we actually won the war, and kept the Union intact."

"At a huge cost of lives and property," said Sam. "And there is still a lot of unrest between the races. The idea that all men or people are created equal, which incidentally should include women as well, has been a very long, slow struggle."

"So you think we should have let them secede and have a country filled with slaves and slaveowners next to our own country?" asked Grant.

"That's a tricky question," said Sam. "You know I don't condone slavery, and we always have to weigh the elements of free choice. A person chooses what they want to be in their life, and chooses their parents. So people choosing to be born to a slave come into this life knowing they will be a slave. Then they have to work within that construct."

"Why would anyone choose to do that?" asked Grant.

"For the same reason they would choose to be a female child born into a family that believes in arranged marriages. There are lots of reasons, and it depends on the lesson that that particular person or spirit wants to learn. And just because someone is born a slave doesn't mean they will stay one."

"You mean they could run away?" asked Grant.

"Sure, or lead a revolt. The best revolts come from within the oppressed group. When a group finds its voice and feels empowered they do more for themselves than if someone else makes a value judgement and tells them how it is going to be," said Sam.

"Can you lead a revolt without any killing?" queried Grant.

"Sure. You yourself know the importance of strategy and tactics. Like the siege of Vicksburg, where you starve out the enemy and cause them to surrender.

I'm not saying that it's good to be the cause of starvation, but that's kinder than killing people," said Sam. "Then again, Lincoln had been working on a plan to pay all of the slaveowners for their slaves, to set them free that way, and then they could stay on as employees. But then Lincoln was killed."

"You think that would have solved the slavery issue peacefully?" asked Grant.

"Maybe," said Sam. "It depends on the reason people have slaves. For some, it was a cheap source of labor, the only way they felt they could afford to do the work on their land. For others it was a power trip, of being able to make other human beings do whatever the master said. And in those cases, if you look at how the master treated his family, he was often dictatorial towards his wife and children as well. And then some people were like Julia, they had grown up with slaves and never even questioned it as an institution, they just accepted it and continued it. People often feel that way about religion-- they just do what their parents did, without thinking about whether it's right or wrong. It's always healthiest to stay centered on what God wants, and to work accordingly. Provided that we don't use God's name in vain, like in the

Crusades, when people went out and killed in the name of religion. Remember, God is the Father of every living being, and doesn't regard one child as better than another."

"So in the Crusades, killing to regain Jerusalem was a false god," said Grant.

"Right. Jerusalem is sacred to many of the world's peoples, and ideally, land should belong to no one. The land belongs to God, or in the Native American way of looking at things, to the Earth Mother. We should use what we need and no more than that. And we need to remember that we can't really own that which isn't humans' right to own."

"But what about property deeds?"

"Invented by humans," said Sam. "It's a power and money thing again. Think how different the world would be if everything were shared, and everyone had what they needed."

"What if people wanted a bigger house?"

"Then they could pay to have one, I suppose, but wouldn't the world be a nicer place if everyone really were equal, and we all had just what we needed? It's something to think about, Ulys." Sam seemed to be straining to hear something. Suddenly, he announced, "I have to go check on something down on earth, so you think about it while I'm gone. I'll see you tomorrow." He gave Grant an encouraging smile. And with that, Sam made his departure, the light fading as he did so.

Chapter 5

Graven Images

"So," said Sam the next day, "Do you know what the second commandment is?"

Grant considered this a moment as he basked in the light and warmth that he always felt when his mentor was near. "Not taking the name of the Lord in vain?"

"Close," replied Sam, with a faint smile. "That's the third commandment." Becoming more serious, he continued, "The second one says 'Thou shalt not make for thyself a graven image, nor any likeness of anything that is in heaven above, or that is in the earth beneath, or that is in the water under the earth; thou shalt not bow down to them or serve them; for I the Lord thy God am a jealous God, visiting the iniquity of the fathers upon the children to the third and fourth generation of those who hateth me, but showing steadfast love to thousands of those who love me and keep my commandments'."

Grant listened with interest. It had been a long, long time since he had heard the entire text of the commandments, let alone given them any thought. But if this was how he was to rid himself of all these ghosts, then he was definitely going to give it his full attention.

"What do you think about this commandment?" asked Sam.

"Well, for starters, I don't have any graven images, at least none that I can think of. I guess you mean that great big golden calf they made in the desert and worshiped back then?"

"That, and similar," said Sam.

"Does it mean not making pictures of God? What about all those famous paintings of Jesus? And religious medallions such as the Catholic soldiers carried?" asked Grant.

Sam nodded. "Those are all very good questions.

In answer to the first, I've never seen anyone paint a picture of God. People seem to understand that God cannot be captured on paper or canvas."

"They claim He's in the shroud of Turin, though," said Grant.

"True, but that isn't God's image, it's Jesus' image. Which brings us to the departing point for some of the Christian religions. There is a strange dichotomy in which they regard Jesus as equal to God, and in some cases greater than God, if you look closely at some of the Catholic prayers. If Jesus equals God, and we'll discuss that in a moment, then there shouldn't be any pictures of him either, let alone people worshiping pictures of Jesus and bowing before them and kissing them, as they do in the Eastern Orthodox churches. In a way, that behavior isn't all that different from worshiping a golden calf, which was a manifestation of shall we say a god that the people back then could relate to."

"Our God, the One True God who created everything," continued Sam, "periodically sends prophets and teachers and messengers to carry His message to humans, so that the people will learn how to walk closer to God's path. But that doesn't mean we should kneel down or bow down and worship the messenger. Yes, we should listen to the messenger, and learn what we can from him or her, but not bow down and worship them as a god. These other people or things are only sent by God to carry the Message, and here I use Message with a capital M."

Grant pondered this for a long moment. "I've been in a number of churches in my life, and they always talk about the Trinity, which is the Father, the Son, and the Holy Ghost," he said. "They are all equal, all parts of the same; at least that's how it's taught."

"But Jesus himself never set out to create a new religion. He was a Jewish rabbi who hoped to bring about some changes in his religion, simple changes. After he died, though, the message he had brought got distorted by his followers, for a variety of reasons, not least of which is that they were human and had a lot of their own issues. Also, some of the biggest proponents of worshiping the messenger had never actually even met Jesus, and so they never heard his teachings spoken in the context they were meant for."

"I know what you mean," said Grant. "You can take the teachings of someone and distort them in ways that person never thought of. I met an interesting soul up here, a physicist of some sort, who told me that he had studied the technology of nuclear power. A lot of what he said was way over my head, since science was never my strong suit, but the gist of it was that he and a group of fellow scientists had taken that knowledge of how to create power, and instead of using it to benefit humanity by making energy for heating houses or something peaceful, they created some sort of an atomic bomb, which was later used in a war. The bomb got dropped on people in Japan and killed tens of thousands of people. Many more were affected by the radioactive fallout this bomb device created. The water and soil were polluted, and deformed children were born. The cattle were deformed and the milk wasn't safe. There have been all kinds of disastrous effects from this bomb, and the fellow I met was just torn with grief that his invention for nuclear power had been used to harm and destroy so many people and beings. In fact, he seemed quite as wretched as me; that's how I first noticed him."

Sam listened as Ulysses spoke. He had heard about the whole atomic bomb debacle. "Yes," said Sam. "I can see how he would be quite miserable. One concept, one invention, and a huge chain reaction of death and destruction. Like war itself, and that event happened in the context of war. It would be so much better if war were just a game people played on a plastic mat with little game pieces, and then the two sides would know who had won, without any sacrifices of human lives. It would be much more humane, and far more sensible and in keeping with God's teachings. But human beings are a stubborn lot," commented Sam.

"It all comes back to the 'false god' concept we talked about the other day," continued Sam. "In the context of World War II, the goal of winning a war and power became the driving forces that allowed people to consider using a dangerous weapon that went against God's commandment that thou shalt not kill. In the interest of winning a war, and quote quickly and easily as I've heard the proponents of the bomb say, these people decided to ignore the fact that the Japanese were just as much God's children as they themselves are. You yourself were a parent; did your children ever fight?"

"Oh, yes," said Grant.

"But you still loved them, and loved them equally, right?" asked Sam.

Grant nodded in agreement. "Absolutely. I tried to never play favorites," he said.

"Well, how would you as a parent have felt if in order to settle an argument, one of your sons stabbed and killed the other?"

"I'd be grief stricken," said Grant. "First at the loss of the son who was killed in such a senseless way, and then the grief of knowing that my other son thought that that was an acceptable way to solve an argument. It would mean that I had failed to teach them properly in some way, I suppose. My goodness, the sheer grief of it all." Ulysses' big expressive blue eyes filled with sorrow and grief.

"You've got it," said Sam. "That's how God felt when the Americans dropped the bomb on Hiroshima. One group of His children killed another group. His grief was immense. For both groups. They missed the message."

Grant nodded. "And when God sent his son Jesus as a messenger, the people killed him. It's really sad," said Grant, "both for Jesus and for God."

"I know," said Sam. "Since I've been up here, learning God's commandments, I am increasingly struck by man's inhumanity to man. Jesus of course was the most highly visible example, that people could kill a simple rabbi for expressing his truth as he saw it, the message from God that he felt called to bring. But everyday on planet earth, there are millions of examples of people being unkind to each other. They insult each other, backstab each other to steal their jobs or break up marriages; they rob and steal and rape and pillage and murder. Every single day on the planet. There's almost always a war going on somewhere on the planet, and people creating weapons of destruction. Then there's all the damage to the planet itself, with pollution and wanton wastage of materials like building thousands of buildings that no one can afford to buy or rent. The buildings sit vacant, the trees have been cut down, and the waters are polluted. People drink or bathe in polluted water, they get sick and they die. They breathe the chemicals that are dumped into the air and they die. The guy who invented asbestos died of the lung disease it causes, and on his death bed, when he knew this and had one last chance to stop the substance, he let it go to market. Many, many more people since him have been affected by asbestosis, and it could have stopped with him. New foods are constantly released by businesses who ignore the dangers of the compounds in the food and foist them on an unsuspecting public. People get sick from these foods, some of which cause awful side effects, and it was all preventable. We need to stop tearing up the farm land to build things, and go back to growing healthy normal food, fresh from Mother Earth as God intended. He gave us all these wonderful gifts, and people abuse His kindness and His gifts. It makes me so sad, and so angry, and there's not much I can do about it," said Sam, sadly.

"If we help one person, and he or she helps another one, it would create a positive chain," said Grant, trying to cheer up his mentor.

"True, but it's so slow. I'd like to see more rapid results, and I think that's what Jesus was thinking when he chose to go to earth to carry God's message to the people. But there's no easy way." Sam fell silent, lost in his own thoughts.

Grant was touched. This was a human side of his teacher. Yes, Sam was smart and caring, but Grant had never seen him get this emotional about a topic before. And since Sam was an angel working for God, God himself must get even more aggravated at the way people behaved. Grant sighed.

After a long while, Sam spoke. "I think the thing that really helps me when I get so frustrated at how people are on earth is the last part of this commandment, where God promises that He will show steadfast love to the thousands who love Him and who keep His commandments. No matter what, He loves us, and if we keep working towards a better world, a better world will eventually occur. It's a promise of hope."

Grant nodded. "I know, and I thank you." He had seen into Sam's soul too and was incredibly moved by what he had seen. The incredible compassion of God and His angels for His beings was just amazing, thought Grant.

And with that, they each drifted off.

A group of slaves floated past Grant and Sam one day. Naked, shackled together, Grant watched as they were led to a stand and auctioned off.

"Where is that?" asked Grant.

"Charleston, South Carolina," replied Sam. "But it went on all over the South, and in other places too. Do you remember writing in your <u>Memoirs</u> the following-- 'As time passes, people, even of the South, will begin to wonder how it was possible that their ancestors ever fought for or justified institutions which acknowledged the right of property in man'."

Grant nodded his head in acknowledgment. "Even though the war was actually fought over a number of things."

"Be that as it may," said Sam, "You and Julia owned slaves. The property of a wife is also the property of her husband, and Julia did not give up her four slaves until the 13th Amendment was ratified in 1865. Missouri was exempt from the Emancipation Proclamation, and it took another year to free the rest of the slaves. She had them the whole time you were fighting for the Union in the Civil War. In fact, your wife used to bring Jule, the children's nurse, who was one of your wife's slaves, with her when she came to visit you in camp."

"But they were hers," said Grant.

"You didn't want to ask, or tell, your wife to give up her slaves and yet you expected that all the slaveholders in the South would give them up?" Sam asked incredulously.

"But Julia was attached to them. She'd known them since her childhood. Her dusky train, as she called them. Used to have far more of them when she was growing up--ten or twelve little black girls that followed her around and did whatever she wanted. Her family loved having slaves. They called it the 'Divine Institution'."

"But that didn't make it right," said Sam. "No human being should be treated as property, as you said in your <u>Memoirs</u>. It cannot be a 'Divine Institution' if it is something that doesn't respect each person as an individual. God made each individual special and unique, not some lesser than others that they should 'serve' others in forced servitude. That their children should be sold and they not able to prevent it. These things and more must needs be on the conscience of all those who participated in this degradation of human beings."

The ghost of Jesse Grant floated by. "I told you not to marry that slaveholder girl. Nothing good could come of one such as her being part of the Grant family. Never could abide slavery myself," he said, sternly. Having spoken his piece, he moved off into the distance.

"Then, of course, there's the Constitution, which says 'One Nation, *Under God*, with Liberty and Justice *For All*'," said Sam. "It was written in 1776, and was meant to apply to everyone. It's a great idea."

"But some of the framers of the constitution, like

Thomas Jefferson, held slaves," protested Grant.

"That's true, and it doesn't make it right. I could also point out that it's interesting that you are <u>defending</u> slavery at this point, as you did by allowing your wife to bring her slave with her into a Union army encampment. Now getting back to Jefferson, let's consider what he helped to write in the Constitution, and compare it with his actual behavior. Jefferson <u>liked</u> having slaves, because he could do as he pleased with them, like that poor Sally Hemings that he kept promising to give her freedom, especially after the children she bore by him. He never did give her the freedom she yearned for, although he did free their children, to the best of my knowledge. Since all People are created equal, according to the Constitution, there was no reason he couldn't have married her, especially since his wife had died."

"What about the miscegenation laws?" asked Grant. "The ones that made it illegal for blacks and whites to have sexual relations."

"Doesn't seem to have worked, does it?" said Sam. "Look around, especially in the South. There are lots of people of mixed blood. The states that were the most opposed to miscegenation often have the most of it.

Like Louisiana. White men set up their mulatto mistresses in houses, and in essence, kept a second family on the side, in addition to the white wife and children they were expected to have. Often the black 'wife' was someone the man truly cared about, but felt he couldn't marry. So instead of just doing the honest thing, and marrying the woman he loved, regardless of color, these men committed adultery, to both wives, which is a far greater sin than marrying a person of another color. God is not any particular color, and when He created all the different colors of people, He didn't make any of them lesser or greater than others, just different. Like all the different flavors of ice cream. Strawberry isn't 'morally superior' to chocolate, for instance."

"I knew of a lot of guys with black mistresses on the side, from the time I was at West Point clear through the Civil War," acknowledged Grant. "So you're saying that slavery could not have been a 'divine institution' because it went against God's view that all people are equal, a view that we as a nation confirm again in our constitution."

"Right," said Sam. "I think you've got it."

Just then the ghost of little Gregorio floated by,

looking reproachfully at Grant.

"Ah, Gregorio," said Sam to Grant, "The little Mexican boy you purchased as a slave during the Mexican War."

"But I let him go when he demanded his freedom," said Grant.

"Although you and Julia resented having to do so, and blamed it on the meddlesome neighbors, rather than looking at the ethics of what you had done," said Sam.

"But lots of people bought Mexican boys and girls when we were there," said Grant.

"This from a man who didn't let his troops steal from the houses in towns they were occupying," said Sam.

"That wouldn't have been right, to steal from people's houses," said Grant.

"But then you're saying that what you did to Gregorio and his parents was right because since he was a 'slave' and you had <u>paid</u> for him, that he was less than human and that you were <u>entitled</u> to do as you pleased."

"But his parents sold him," said Grant.

"Just because something is for sale, people don't need to buy it. Eliminate demand, and supply will stop. His parents were poverty-stricken, and we cannot presume to know their motives without talking to them directly. They must answer for their actions, as must all parents who would do that to a child. But getting back to you, you, Ulysses Grant, did not need to purchase a slave."

"I know," said Grant. "At the time, I could even imagine my father's voice saying 'Don't do it. It's wrong. Having slaves is wrong.' But it was such a small sum of money really. So what do I do now? How do I make amends to him? I can't go back and undo the whole thing," Grant said to his mentor.

"You could begin by apologizing for participating in his enslavement, and for using him as property," suggested Sam. "Speak from your heart, and let the words flow."

Grant hung his head. "I'm too ashamed," he said.

"Personally, I would begin my apology, and see what I could do to make amends," said Sam. "I know it seems hard to do, for apologizing is something you've never been very good at, but Gregorio is a nice boy. He deserved better than his lot in life. He certainly deserves an apology, at the very least."

"Can't it wait?" asked Grant.

"It could," said Sam, "But the longer you wait, the

tougher it gets, not easier. Besides, you can't mess it up. You already had your impact on his life, and now it's time to make amends. Go, try."

Grant reluctantly floated over to the Mexican boy. Gregorio had been killed in a fight with his next master, and still looked as young as he had when he worked for the Grants.

"Hello," said Ulysses.

Gregorio eyed him warily.

"I came to tell you I'm sorry for everything that happened between us, me buying you and taking you away from your parents, who were desperate for the money. It doesn't make it right, and I'm sorry."

"Are you really sorry," said Gregorio, "Or just saying it because he told you to?" Gregorio pointed to where Sam was waiting in the background.

"Both," admitted Grant.

They looked at each other and laughed, feeling some of the tension dissipate.

"I knew that because there are people I need to deal with here in order to be free and move on," said Gregorio.

"Like who?" asked Grant, curious.

"Like my parents. I don't understand how some-one could sell off their child, no matter how poor they are. There are always other choices. I guess they never loved me, that I was just a piece of property to them," said the Mexican boy.

Grant felt the sorrow and desolation of the boy's experience. He thought about his own sons, and how he would never have sold them.

"You didn't watch us too well, either, father," said young Fred as he materialized next to Gregorio. The other two looked at this new arrival in surprise.

"Remember when you let me come with you to camp at the start of the Civil War, and then when you and the regiment were to move on, you decided to send me home by myself? You didn't wait until the letter from Mother, where she advised you to keep me in your sight until you yourself could see me home. Nooo. So you gave me money to go home by water, on a little boat up the Mississippi, and sent some sergeant to accompany me to the dock," said Grant's son Fred.

Grant nodded as he listened to his eldest son, never suspecting what came next.

"We got to the dock, but it was over an hour 'til

the boat would leave, so the sergeant took me into this bar. It was filthy, with roaches, and garbage on the floor. He insisted I drink a glass of alcohol, and he had some too. Next thing I knew, he was assaulting me, and took all my money. So I had to walk home, all seventeen miles. Took me fifteen hours, but I was too scared to stop along the way."

"My God, my poor son," exclaimed Grant. "Why didn't you come back to the barracks and tell me?"

"I was too ashamed, and the sergeant threatened to kill me if I told anyone. Said he'd destroy your career too, and I couldn't let that happen," said Fred.

"I remember the letter Julia sent me after you arrived home," said Grant, reflecting on this. "She said you arrived exhausted, bedraggled and depressed, after walking the entire way home. I couldn't figure out why you'd walked when I gave you money for the boat, but I figured your mother was confused."

Gregorio came over to Fred and gave him a hug. "You poor boy. I know how you feel," he said to Fred.

On hearing this, Grant was even more ashamed of his early behavior toward Gregorio. And that such a thing could have happened to his own son, his flesh and blood, why, it made him so angry he was ready to go find that sergeant and rip him limb from limb.

Sam came over to intervene at this point. "But it's just as much your fault as that sergeant's," he said to Grant. "Was that how a good father would have acted, trusting the care of his young son to an unknown man? What was more important--your time, or seeing your son safely back home? You had many other choices, including not taking him with you to camp in the first place, taking him home yourself, or keeping him with you, as Julia suggested. What was more important?"

Grant pondered this. "I wanted to relieve what I supposed was Mrs. Grant's great anxiety for one so young going into danger," he said. "I had no idea this would happen. Am I responsible for mistakes of omission such as this, as well as acts of commission, like with Gregorio?" he asked Sam. *Strange thing to be discussing,* thought Grant, *but we're all men here.*

Sam nodded. "Any time you fail to consider the consequences of your actions and their impact on other people, yes, you are responsible. We all need to think ahead, and consider all the possibilities, always within the framework of What does God want me to do? What would be most in keeping with God's teachings?"

The other three ghosts all nodded. Grant spoke next, reaching out towards both boys, tears filling his large blue eyes. "I am so sorry. I hope you can both find it in your hearts to forgive me. I know now that what I did in each of your lives was wrong, and stupidity cannot be my defense. But I will do whatever I can to make it up to both of you, from this point forward, and I shall personally vow to take action in my next lifetime to prevent abuse against children, especially boys, since people don't think that such things happen to boys."

"Thank you, sir," said Gregorio.

As Gregorio floated off, Grant hoped that it would not be the last time he ever saw the boy. There was something about the boy that he had always liked, a nobleness of spirit, and Grant wanted to do all that he could to help Gregorio move on. It was the least he could do, reflected Grant.

"So you and Gregorio..." said Fred. "You mean like that sergeant and me? How could you? What kind of animal are you?" Fred floated off in a huff.

Sam addressed Grant. "This will sort itself out in time. You need to think about things, and also to allow time to begin to heal these wounds. And, your idea about doing something constructive to stop these sort of things is a good idea." And with that, Sam too floated off into the ether, leaving Grant lots of time to think.

The ghostly form of a priest floated into Grant's view one day. He spoke no English, only Spanish. Something about him was familiar, thought Grant. Dash it all, these priests all look alike, in their black outfits and white collars.

"San Cosme," said Sam as he arrived on the scene, surrounded by light. "It's the priest from the church in San Cosme, during the Mexican War."

"I didn't go to Church much during the war," said Grant. "And if I had gone, it would have been to a

Methodist service."

"You didn't go to his church for religious worship," said Sam. "Today we're talking about 'Remember the Sabbath Day and keep it holy', and also about keeping holy all those things which are by nature holy, such as churches. The good Padre here has consented to help me with today's lesson, for the events which transpired at your hands have troubled him for many years. Think. Can you remember what you did at the church there?"

Grant thought. Suddenly he remembered that as a result of his actions at the church General Worth himself had commended Grant. "I had my men carry a howitzer up to the belfry and used it to fire at the enemy."

"And was the priest glad to help you or did he try to give you the message that what you were about to do was wrong and disrespectful of God?" asked Sam.

"He refused to admit us," replied Grant truthfully. "He didn't speak any English, and I used the little bit of Spanish that I knew to tell him that if he didn't let us in, then I would break the door down and come in anyhow, destroying property if he obstructed me. I conveyed that it was to his advantage to let me do as I wished, for I intended to go in whether he consented or not. I also told him that his cooperation would keep him from being taken prisoner, at least for the moment."

"So, let's review a moment," said Sam. "You broke in to the good Padre's church, told him you were coming in and if he obstructed you then his property would be destroyed and he'd be taken prisoner, and then you had a howitzer, an instrument of death and destruction, placed in the belfry of the church were the bells are that announce times of worship, among other things. Then you used your position in a house of worship to shoot at people for the purpose of harming them. From a church, a place of safe harbor in all ages and in all nationalities, a peaceful sanctuary. How could you deface a place of worship in such a manner? By whose authority did you do this?"

"My own," admitted Grant. "It was a great idea. It was the last place anyone thought to look for a cannon."

"But it was morally repugnant," said Sam. "The priest tried to convey that to you, but you didn't want to understand the message he was trying to send your spirit. The city authorities even sent a delegation to General Scott to ask for an armistice and that Church property be respected."

"Which General Scott declined to do," said Grant, with a smirk.

"But it doesn't make what you did right. God, and the concept of doing the right thing, are higher orders than the false gods of winning and power. Would anything have been different in the war if Ulysses Grant hadn't commandeered a church?" asked Sam.

"We wouldn't have won as easily," said Grant.

"But your soul would have been in better shape," said Sam. "And you would have had one less ghost to deal with, and one less commandment to relearn. Moral principle or imperative is always more important than the battles that man devises."

Sam turned to the ghost of the Padre. "You may go now," he said kindly. "I appreciate your help. There was nothing you could have done to stop this man, for he was determined to take those actions that occurred that day. You did your duty as a humble servant of God by trying to prevent the officer's entry into the church. You have prayed for his soul, as I have on many occasions. There is nothing more you could have done, and you need hold no further guilt or worry on this matter. That must be borne by the one who chose the course of action, and he and I will discuss this further later. Go in peace, and God Bless You, Padre."

There was a visible lightening of the specter's aura, and then he was gone. Not flown off, but gone.

"Where did he go?" asked Grant.

His mentor Sam replied, "His last worry is now resolved. He finally felt free to go on to heaven. He was a good priest and it's not his fault that you decided to commandeer his church to use for violent purposes."

"So," said Grant, "If he went to heaven, is this hell?"

"The priest didn't do anything terrible enough to warrant a trip to hell. He just failed to stop what to many people was a 'madman'," said Sam.

"So, if this isn't heaven and it isn't hell, where am I? Do you live here, too?" asked Grant.

"Most of the time," replied Sam. "I've had a few other lifetimes on earth since the one I messed up in ancient Greece. I had to learn a lot of the same lessons that I'm teaching you now."

"How did you mess up?" asked Grant. "You know so much; you are so wise. I can't imagine you making the same kinds of mistakes that I did."

Sam sighed. "If you only knew."

"You know all about me," pointed out Grant. "Tell me about you."

Sam considered a moment. "Like you, I used to drink. In fact, I killed some of my best friends when I was drunk. My father and I united the Greek city states by force. Talk about a father's career plans for his son. And then, as if that wasn't enough, we wiped out the Persian Empire." Sam appeared lost in thought.

A light went on in Grant's head. This must be Alexander the Great, he thought. Wow! One of my heroes. This guy was one of the most amazing military commanders ever.

Sam looked at Grant, aware of his thoughts, and nodded, looking very sad. Then Sam continued, "A helper spirit came to me after I died, just like I came to you. And it took me a long time to accept his help. Like you, I had to hit rock bottom before I could look at my actions. Every day, since that point, I try to grow closer toward the light."

"What happened to your helper?" asked Grant, fascinated that other military people who he had so greatly admired had been through some of the same things he had.

"He's in heaven, now," said Sam. "And someday, I will be too. Part of how we demonstrate we're ready to go there is when we understand God's teachings well enough to teach them to others. And not the dogma that a lot of fundamentalist groups on earth <u>say</u> are God's teachings. God's teachings are very simple, and to find them you need to look at all the different faiths, for the same basic principles appear over and over, like 'Love One Another as I Have Loved You'. The Ten Commandments are a very clear statement, and the Eastern religions have a clear concept on what happens to the soul, in terms of reincarnation, and karma, and that sort of thing. So, when I've clearly mastered this material, I get to move on."

"And your sins are forgiven, like killing your best friends and wiping out an entire Empire?" asked Grant, amazed.

"God is infinitely loving and compassionate. He knew that when He gave us the ability to do as we wanted so that we could learn what we needed to, that we might make unfortunate choices. But, as I always tell you, every choice has a consequence, even if we don't realize it at the time. We always have to answer for the choices we make and realize which choices were the better moral imperative. So no, we don't have to live a perfect life, for man by nature is imperfect, and God loves all His creations, flaws and all. But we do have to come to a full understanding of God's teachings. And some of us are slower learners than others."

"But if God created Man in His own image, how come we're not perfect?" asked Grant.

"That's a great question," replied Sam. "A bunch of us who are into philosophy have debated that one for centuries. But we're only the second draft, anyhow. The first time God made people, they were such a corrupt lot that He got rid of them all, with the Great Flood. He saved Noah and Noah's family, to use the Judeo-Christian version of the story and that's where the second draft comes from. Stories about the Great Flood are found in most cultures on Earth."

"Oh," said Grant. "But if God is the Creator, how come we're not all perfect?"

"Well," said Sam, "I figure it's like creating art. Sometimes, you create a painting and it's beautiful. Other times, you can see the flaws, but it's basically okay; it's not your best work, but it's not garbage either. And sometimes, you paint something and it just comes out so bad, it's better to just throw it away and start over. That's how it is for God, who has created so many things. But He always loves us, no matter what, and He feels bad when a work has to go in the trash, so to speak. Like the story where He created the first rainbow as a sign that he would never do anything so drastic again, after the Noah episode. God has kept that promise, and so He's stuck with the current batch of humans. Now He has to find ways to educate these humans, to help them get back on track." And with that, Sam graciously took his leave, and faded off into the ether.

Chapter Eight

Honor Thy Father and Thy Mother

"Okay," said Sam, "let's talk about the Big War today, the one that started in 1861. Let's go back in time to the Ulysses you were back then, a man of thirty-nine. What are your thoughts?"

"I feel really bad and I cannot turn back," answered Grant. "One of my superstitions has always been that when I start to go anywhere or to do anything, not to turn back or stop until the thing intended is accomplished."

Sam nodded. "Let's go back in time to the

excitement in Galena, at the start of the War of the Rebellion. When you volunteered for the war."

Grant smiled at the memory. "I wrote to the Adjutant General of the Army."

"Goodness, man, what were you thinking?" said Sam. "You hated the Army, hated the bloodshed of combat, the boredom in between. You yearned to be home with Julia and the children. So, you finally get home, you're leading as normal a life as possible, and what do you do? You try to sign up for more of the same that almost destroyed you."

"But he never responded to my letter," Grant pointed out. "They found it years later when someone was cleaning out his office. It had never been filed."

"And you didn't get the hint," said Sam. "So then you went to see General McClellan. You hoped he'd offer you a position on his staff. No surprise that he wouldn't see you, although you tried for two days. You still didn't get it."

"You mean I wasn't supposed to get into the Army at that point? But Julia's angel said I was destined for greatness."

"Let's deal with those comments in order," said

Sam. "First, <u>your</u> angels, including myself, did everything we could to stop you from going back into a situation that would be bad for you. Unlike you, <u>we</u> knew that war results in killing, which is against God's commandments. But no, you continued to try to join the Army, despite your having resigned to avoid that court-martial for being drunk on duty."

Grant looked confused.

"You know the old saying--Be careful what you wish for, because you just might get it?" Sam asked.

Grant nodded.

"Well, that's what happened. You got what you persisted in asking for, and a whole lot more came with it. You were responsible for the deaths of tens of thousands of men, and it's caused you 133 years of misery since the time it happened."

Grant pondered this as he stroked his beard, how his guardian helper had tried to prevent the chain of events that had led to his present predicament, and how he, Grant, had been so bent on doing what <u>he</u> wanted that he'd ignored all the signs.

Aware of Grant's thoughts, Sam commented, "And you didn't even ask Julia how she felt about you going back into the Army, especially to destroy the institution of slavery that she and her family held so dear."

Grant acknowledged the truth of that remark.

"You know, for a man who said he never likes to retrace his path, this is one time you went right back to an old road," Sam pointed out.

"I joined as a Colonel, a higher rank," said Grant as he denied his guardian spirit's accusation.

"But it was the Army all over again," said Sam. "Parties and drinking with the officers. Trying to ignore the sorrow. Not understanding that yes, you could have had the life you had dreamed of in the past. You and Julia and the children could have moved out West and ignored the whole Rebellion. You could have been a farmer, or a businessman. Anything, just no more bloodshed."

"Well what about Julia's angel telling her I was destined for greatness?" asked Grant, a testy note in his voice.

"That happened because she was unhappy with the cabin you built, Hardscrabble, and she was depressed. You could have avoided all that grief by asking her what kind of house she wanted in the first place. She preferred Wish-ton-Wish, the house you eventually bought from her brother. That was elegant, much more her style. It's nice that you built a house yourself, but you could have eliminated a lot of aggravation and hurt feelings by figuring out what kind of house would be best for both of you. Like the old saying, 'measure twice, cut once'. To answer the greatness issue, though, there are many ways in which people achieve 'greatness'. Some become famous and live their life in the public eye, which comes with its own price tag, as you well know."

"<u>Personal</u> greatness, though," continued Sam, "is living your life as close to the path of God as possible, to live a fulfilling and peaceful life, honoring God's commandments. To be the kindest and best person we possibly can, not necessarily the richest or most famous."

Sam observed Grant, and the fact that Ulysses seemed somewhat lost in this logic. Sam decided to approach the topic from another direction to add clarity.

"Let's consider some of the men besides your own biological father that you have regarded as father figures in your most recent lifetime," suggested Sam.

"Okay," said Grant. "That's easy. General Taylor, you know, Zachary Taylor, who eventually became President, and my old mentor Thomas Hamer."

"Great," said Sam. "Let's start with General Taylor and see what we can learn about being a good father from him."

"Ah, General Taylor," said Grant, smiling. "Now there's a man I admire. No soldier could face either danger or responsibility more calmly than he did. It's a gift he had. And he never troubled the administration with his demands; he just did the best he could with the means he had been given. He never made any great show or parade, either of uniform or retinue, not like a lot of other commanding officers. He dressed plainly, rarely wearing anything in the field to indicate his rank or even that he was an officer, but he was known to every soldier in his army and was respected by all."

"Okay," said Sam. "So some of the things that you admired about him was that he did the best with what he had, he was brave, and he was a simple man, not one for fancy dress and fanfare. Fair summary?"

Grant nodded.

"Did you ever consider why he didn't like to wear his uniform?" asked Sam. "Considering that you didn't like to either."

"Hmmm," said Grant. "I thought it was because

he wasn't showy."

"Maybe he wasn't comfortable in the Army either. Choosing to not wear a uniform that everyone is required to wear is a way of making a statement, however subtle. You yourself made this statement many times in your lifetime," said Sam.

"I never thought about how he felt about the Army. Maybe that's why he tried to do everything with as little bloodshed as possible. People used to get on his case because they thought he was too lenient. I was far stricter," said Grant.

"What do you suppose he was like as a father?"

"I don't know," said Grant. "He was more soft-spoken than my father, that's for sure. I guess he wasn't home much, though, since he was in the Army, like I was."

"Well, one of things you admired was that he was known to every man in the Army. If we apply that to civilian life, then a good father would be known to every person in his home and family," said Sam.

"My family all knew me," said Grant.

"I don't think so," said Sam. "You were away in California for two years before you ever even saw Ulysses

Jr. In fact, your son Fred at age three had no idea of what his father even looked like. One time, you sent a friend with some letters to your wife, and she invited the friend to stay for supper. Fred stared at him throughout the meal and finally said, "Mamma, is that ugly man my pappa?" A long discussion ensued, for the man was not young Fred's pappa, and he had taken a bit of offence at being called ugly."

"Oh dear," said Grant, looking chagrined. "I had no idea."

"And right after Ulysses Jr. was born, Julia's sisters told her she should name him Telemachus, for she would have to call on her little Telemachus to find and bring back to her the wandering Ulysses," said Sam.

"Ouch," said Grant.

"Julia had always told the children how wonderful and brave you were, and when you came back from California, all you did was drink. She was embarrassed that the way she remembered you was not at all like the way the children saw their pappa act."

"I remember that," said Grant. "Julia never reproached me about my drinking except that one time. I had never really considered her or the children in my drinking. I drank to forget; I drank because I was bored; and I drank so I wouldn't have the shakes. But I never considered Julia or the children until that one episode. After that, I took the Temperance pledge, but as we've discussed, I fell back to my old ways."

"So another characteristic of a good father would be a man who considers the wishes and needs of others, particularly his wife and children. For instance, had Jesse considered your personality and skills and what would have been best for you, he would have realized that you would have fared better as a professor, and sent you to a non-military college. Or even trained you to be a farmer. A good father should place the child's needs and wishes ahead of his own, so that he can help his child to become the best person he possibly can, to lead a pleasant and fulfilling life," said Sam.

"I guess the thing that most struck me about my mentor, Thomas Hamer, was how little control we have over our own destiny," said Grant. "He was the member of Congress who gave me the appointment to West Point. Later, he was a major with an Ohio regiment who joined us at Matamoras. He was one of the ablest men Ohio ever produced, in the prime of his life, and due to be appointed brigadier general. There was even talk of him becoming President one day. But he was taken ill before Monterrey and died within a few days. He never got to be President."

"But being President is not necessarily the be-all and end-all of someone's existence. You yourself commented on many occasions how you couldn't wait to be out of the White House and rid of the responsibility of being President," said Sam.

"I know," said Grant. "I even used my favorite quote to start my memoirs--Man proposes and God disposes. There are but few important events in the affairs of men brought about by their own choice."

"Well," said Sam, "we need to be careful what we ask for. You asked God to let you win the War of the Rebellion. And He did, at a huge cost to your spirit. You were determined, and you let your superstition about not turning back rule you, with major consequences from an ethical point of view."

"Now, work with me here, Grant," continued Sam. "What would have happened if you had simply said <u>No</u>; No to military school, No to joining the Army; No to the Mexican War; No to the War of the Rebellion. Basically, No as soon as you realized that war was wrong, that people were going to get killed and that killing was not a good thing. What would have happened, if anything?"

"My father would have died," said Grant, automatically.

"In what way?" asked Sam. "He wasn't on the battlefield in any way. Do you mean he would literally have died, and hence the superstition, like 'Step on a crack and you'll break your mother's back', that old rhyme from grammar school? Or do you mean he would have died metaphorically, as in a part of him died."

Grant considered this for a long moment as he stroked his beard. "Both, I think. His dream was for me to be a military man. When my father wrote to Thomas Hamer to get me into West Point, I originally told him, my father that is, that I wouldn't go. But he went on and on, and eventually I decided to go. That's what good sons do."

"Okay," said Sam, "But what about <u>you</u>? Your father didn't have to live with the spirits of those sixty thousand men who got massacred. <u>You</u> carried that burden. <u>You</u> could have stopped at any point. Yet you didn't."

"I would have turned and run and hid, and cried,

the way little Hiram did, before he learned that men can't do that."

"But," said Sam, "<u>you</u> have a softer side. When you were supposed to be studying at West Point, you were reading romance novels, of all things."

Grant sighed. "I had to be tough. It's like that saying a surgeon I met recently said--'A surgeon may be wrong but he is never in doubt.' Of course, he's here as a ghost because he cut the wrong leg off of that one patient of his, and the patient's husband shot him."

"Okay," said Sam, "let's say as a hypothetical that you ran off and quit the army, as soon as you realized what it would entail."

"They would have court-martialed me or maybe even shot me," said Grant.

"Let's say, then, for the sake of argument, that you left West Point."

A smile lit up Grant's face, and he appeared to blossom, visibly growing lighter. Happy and carefree, the way he had never been in life but had always yearned to be. "I'd have been....<u>free</u>. My God, the greatest feeling in the world. To be free. It's like floating. I wish I could just hang onto this feeling."

"You will, someday. It starts a little at a time, working things through, finding peace and happiness. Sifting through all the painful things as we get to them, looking for the little kernel of knowledge tucked away in even the worst of events. So yes, you will feel this way again," assured Sam.

"I guess at some level, I knew that freedom was there. I couldn't grab it for me, but I worked to give those slaves their freedom."

"But you were a slave too," said Sam gently. "You were a slave to your father's ambitions for you, to your ideas of what a 'good son' should do."

"But isn't that what a good son _is_ supposed to do?"

"You're a father, and you have sons. Is this what you would want for your son?"

"No, I'd want him to be happy, to have a job he was happy to go to every day of his life."

"Exactly," said Sam. "If you and Julia had wanted Jessie to be a doctor, and Jessie hated the sight of sick people, would it have been right to insist he go to medical school, and to badger him that as a 'good son' he should go there?"

"No," said Grant.

"Right," said Sam. "And you hated to hurt living things. You refused to hunt. You hated to see any living thing in pain."

Grant's voice dropped down to a whisper. "All those years of my life. All that pain. To be someone I thought I should be, because that's what someone else wanted me to be, expected me to be. To not have been who or what I wanted to be." He cried, softly. "No one even considered what I wanted."

"Not even you," said Sam, gently. "That's part of the beauty of life. God gives us the freedom to be anything we want to be, so that we can experience things and learn what we need to learn or want to learn."

"So I chose to be a good son, rather than choosing to follow my own dreams. Must have been so long ago, I can't even think what it is I would have wanted to be. Something simple, I suppose, maybe work in the leather shop like my brothers or be a professor of mathematics," said Grant.

"You were a good son, but to the wrong father perhaps."

"What do you mean?" asked Grant.

"You have two fathers, the father you were born to in this life, and your Heavenly Father, God. Being a good son to Jesse Grant is a very different thing than being a good son to God."

"In what way?" asked Grant.

"One of God's commandments is 'Thou Shalt Not Kill.' Your father Jesse was a strict Methodist. He knew the commandments, but his wish for you to be a military man, a great leader, was stronger. And to be a great military man, you had to ignore a few of the commandments. Like Thou Shalt Not Kill. <u>Military</u> people <u>kill</u>; it's part of the gig. But you, my gentle Hiram Ulysses, didn't even <u>hunt</u>. You knew, deep in your soul, that hunting was wrong. You even went around in the Big War unarmed."

"He didn't choose that badly for me," said Grant, on his father's behalf. "I had prestige, a steady job, power, and eventually the admiration of the nation."

"And at a high cost. Young Hiram Ulysses didn't believe in killing. You came into this last lifetime knowing that killing was wrong. But you got conflicted with the Honor thy father and mother commandment. You decided that in order to honor your father in this lifetime, you had to kill. You felt you had to break one commandment in order to keep another. What do you think about that?"

"Casualties are a part of war, that's what they said in college," replied Grant.

"That's what they've been saying since the Crusades, in the medieval period. God created all people, be they Saracen or Jew or Christian, and yet these Christians actually thought God wanted them to go out and massacre tens of thousands of people, people that God had lovingly created in His own image, sons and daughters and husbands and wives and parents. The only 'crime' of all those innocent people slaughtered was the religion to which they belonged, the way in which they prayed and honored God."

Grant listened intently.

Sam continued, "So, military people also ignore the first commandment, that there is One God. Just as all the people in the Crusades worshiped the same God but in different ways, the Northerners and the Southerners all worship the same God too. For that matter, you all bleed the same color, red, not blue or gray."

Grant stroked his beard, pensive. This was indeed a different way of looking at things, he reflected.

"God, the Father of All Beings, does not want His children to kill. He gives them choices, and also gives them a set of guidelines so that they may make good choices. You do not have to disregard one commandment to fulfill another. You can still honor and respect your parents without pursuing a course they set for you, if you know that that course deviates from God's wishes for us."

"But wouldn't God want me to have fame and prestige and a steady job with which to support my family?" asked Grant.

"Let's divide up those issues for the sake of discussion," suggested Sam. "I would agree that God wants you to have a job so that you can support your family. We've talked about fame and prestige and power before, and those are false gods. You don't _need_ fame or prestige or power in order to survive, the way you need food to eat and a roof over your head. And the cost of the career you went into at your father's behest was very high."

"In what way?" asked Grant. "I got paid to do the job."

"The emotional cost, Ulys. The repercussions of your actions. The Army of the Potomac was slaughtered

under your direction. Think of the individuals involved--
the boys and men who were killed, their widows, their
children, their parents. The Jews you threw out of the
Army during that governmental order you issued. And
beyond all that, the cost of your own hopes and dreams,
the loss of your freedom to be whatever you wanted to
be."

In that moment, Grant saw with clarity the true
cost he had paid for his father's decision to send him to
West Point, and his own lack of moral courage to say no
and mean it, or to get lost on the way to the Academy, or
to flunk out, as so many of his fellow students had, some
on purpose, he was sure of it. Now he knew why they had
done that, for at the time it had seemed inconceivable. But
the freedom to live one's life the way one thought was
right, not the way one's parents thought, that would have
been the ultimate luxury. And it was a gift that God had
given him, as He gave all His children. Two fathers--Jesse
and God. Why had he never realized this before now?
Grant pondered this for a long while.

The next day, Grant was ready for Sam with a
question.

"Okay," said Sam, "Go ahead, ask whatever you like."

"If I hadn't gone to West Point, as my father wanted me to, how could I be honoring my father and mother, like the commandment says? Wouldn't that have been dishonoring my parents and their wishes?"

"Let's explore what 'honor' means," said Sam. "It means to treat them with respect. Not to slavishly follow their every whim, especially if their whim or wish conflicts with one of God's teachings. God is your Father through <u>all</u> of your lifetimes, and Jesse and Hannah were your parents for only <u>one</u> lifetime. Sometimes, though, children have to do what their parents say, in order to survive. This happens when children are still dependent. Once you can function on your own, then you are free to make your own choices."

Sam continued, "As an adult, you can be who <u>you</u> want to be and still regard the parents who gave birth to you with kindness, respect and affection. You are their equal, in addition to being their son, for everyone is equal in God's eyes."

"So there are really two levels to consider here," said Grant, putting it into mathematical terms. "Jesse and

Hannah were my parents in this lifetime, and I was to love and honor and respect them, but God as my Father is a stronger force, a larger equation."

Sam nodded.

"But what about guilt?" asked Grant. "I felt so guilty at the thought of not doing what my parents wanted me to do."

"But it was you who had to live with the consequences of your/their choice," said Sam. "So it would have been alright for you to make your own choice about going to West Point. The long-term consequences were of far greater significance than short-term guilt."

"So how do you interpret the commandment to Honor Thy father and Thy mother?" asked Grant with interest.

"Your parents were chosen because of the lessons you wanted to learn from them. Each parent has his or her own unique perspective to transmit. Your parents are also on their own paths to God, and they move along their respective paths at their own pace. We must honor that fact and learn to accept them as the unique individuals they are, with their own good points and bad points. They are not just our parents; they are children of the same God, and that makes them a spiritual brother and sister to us, if you will," explained Sam.

Grant nodded, listening intently.

"The other important issue about our parents," continued Sam, "is that we must honor the beauty of creation, the beauty of the process by which two people can give life to another being, which is a tiny sampling of the work of God. Just as God created the universe, your parents created you."

"Which is another example of the micro-cosm/macrocosm scale of looking at things," said Grant, with enthusiasm. "I'm beginning to understand this concept. I can see it!"

"So," said Sam, "There is a spark of divinity in all parents as they bring children into the world. It's a chance for them to experience the joy of creating, of making a new creation and watching it grow and develop. Parents can learn from their children, not just teach them."

"Since they are all on their own paths to God, they all have things to learn," said Grant, smiling. "I wish I had known all this years ago. My life would have been so different."

Sam nodded. "But the important thing is that you

are learning it now, and you will take this knowledge with you into your next cycle of growth."

Grant sat back to rest and relax and think about the beauty of a world in which all human beings, especially parents and children, were equal.

Chapter 9

Thou Shalt Not Kill

"Today we're going to tackle a very difficult topic," announced Sam. "We're going to talk about the commandment that says Thou Shalt Not Kill. What makes it really tricky is the fact that you were in the military. We've touched on this issue before, in terms of honoring your father, but we haven't considered some of the related issues, and we haven't begun to touch the emotions about these actions, emotions that you've suppressed for all these years. Ghosts all have a purpose, and most of yours are related to the issue of killing."

Sam continued, "I myself was a military leader, too, if that makes this any easier for you, so I know where you are coming from on these issues. But I work for God now, and not for a country or my father or any one else, and I'm going to help you explore this issue the same way that my guardian spirit helped me. Okay?"

Grant nodded. He reflected that it was very thoughtful of Sam to preface the discussion so gently, and it reminded him of the doctor's tone of voice before they biopsied his throat "lesion". Something painful is about to occur, but he's going to help me get through it. Grant took a deep breath, as if he were about to plunge into a pool of icy water. This was indeed where most of the ghosts were, just as his mentor had said. The lessons he had learned this far had taught him much, but the ghosts, by and large, were from this department. Grant figured this was like a muddy creek, something you just had to go through to get to the other side.

"Let's start by looking at young Hiram Ulysses Grant," began Sam. "You hated the idea of killing, and that's why you didn't want to go into your father's tannery business. In fact, during the Civil War, you didn't even carry a weapon."

Sam opened an old leather-bound book and continued, "If we look at your memoirs, you once said, 'I do not believe I ever would have the courage to fight a duel. If any man should wrong me to the extent of my being willing to kill him, I would not be willing to give him the choice of weapons with which it should be done, and of the time, place and distance separating us, when I executed him. If I should do another such a wrong as to justify him killing me, I would make any reasonable atonement within my power, if convinced of the wrong done'."

Grant nodded as he remembered writing that in his chapter on Camp Salubrity in his <u>Memoirs</u>.

"I see by that point a divided Ulysses," commented Sam. "On one hand, you say you would not have the courage to fight a duel. You say that you would do everything possible to atone for whatever you did wrong if you made someone upset enough to want to kill you. On the other hand, you add a smug comment that it would be <u>if</u> you were convinced of the wrong done, and that's often shaky ground. To your credit, you are working on learning what exactly is wrong and how to decide if things are right or wrong for yourself. Then you calmly mentioned executing the other person in the duel. Not a trace of emotion in your tone. Just like when you calmly mentioned the shot that took off Major Albertis' head. A particularly gory detail, and yet you described it without any sense of the horror it engenders in those who witnessed it."

"So I wasn't a good writer," said Grant.

"No, I think you were a pretty good writer," said Sam. "But the emotional part of these issues you kept carefully locked away somehow, or you couldn't and wouldn't have done that which you did during the two wars you served in. You described your troops in completely dispassionate terms as well. In your memoirs, you wrote, 'Some commanders can move troops so as to get the maximum distance out of them without fatigue, while others can wear them out in a few days without accomplishing so much'."

"I was talking about General Worth," said Ulys.

"I know," said Sam. "Remember, I read the book, both volumes of it. But the point is that it sounds like you are discussing shoes, not people. Getting the maximum use out of something is a characteristic we apply to clothing or shoes, not to a human. They were people.

Each and every one of those 'troops' was a human being, with a family and feelings and needs and wants and hopes and dreams. So we're going to talk to a few now."

"Uh oh," thought Grant. He felt a sensation of fear grip him in the pit of his stomach, as if someone had punched him there.

Major Albertis loomed into view, half his head missing. "It hurts like hell," he said. "It hurts like hell. We should never have gone to war. Dumbest thing I ever did. I had no idea it would end like this." He floated away, muttering "Gotta find the rest of my head."

"Then there was the whole episode with Harris, at Florida, Missouri, at the start of the War of the Rebellion, as you called it," said Sam. "Let's look at how you described the conflict. 'I kept my men in the ranks...my heart kept getting higher and higher until it felt to me as though it was in my throat. I would have given anything then to have been back in Illinois, but I had not the moral courage to halt and consider what to do; I kept right on. When we reached a point from which the valley below was in full view I halted. The place where Harris had been encamped a few days before was still there and the marks of a recent encampment were plainly visible, but the troops were gone. My heart resumed its place. It occurred to me at once that Harris had been as much afraid of me as I had been of him. This was a view of the question I had never taken before; but it was one I never forgot afterwards. From that event to the close of the war, I never experienced trepidation upon confronting an enemy, though I always felt more or less anxiety. I never forgot that he had as much reason to fear my forces as I had his. The lesson was valuable'."

Sam closed the old book. "Here you finally acknowledged your human emotions, the very real fear a person would have when there is the possibility of being shot at and killed. And instead of valuing this very normal fear of death, and rethinking your decision to be a part of the military, you decided that the lesson meant that you didn't need to be afraid to do whatever <u>you</u> wanted to do in battle since <u>the other side</u> was afraid. Problem is, your men were afraid, and you should have been too. Fear of being killed and of killing is normal, because it keeps us from going against God's commandment that we are not to kill. No one should deliberately go into a situation of 'kill or be killed.' That's a terrible thing to put onto all the innocent boys who came at their country's call to defend the Union. I'm sure many of them didn't realize they would be killed, or that they'd see so many of their friends and neighbors and relatives killed, or that they'd be fighting against people who were their neighbors and friends and relatives. 'And they shall beat their swords into plowshares.' Peace and harmony is a better way to go, talking things out, remembering our shared humanity, that we are all Children of the Same God. Not killing."

Grant nodded, appearing lost in thought.

"One of things that amazes me is that you knew how bloody and awful war is, from your experiences in the Mexican War. You had felt that that war was unnecessary. You had seen the deaths at Chapultepec and other places. Then _why_ did you reenlist in the Civil War? While it was generally your superiors who were morally responsible for the injuries and deaths on both sides in the Mexican War, it was _your_ moral responsibility in the Civil War, since _you_ were in charge."

"Several reasons, I suppose," said Grant, thoughtfully stroking his beard. "I was bored working with my brother in Galena, although you would probably say that boredom was a sign that I was on the right track and doing the right thing." He looked over at Sam, who nodded.

"And I wasn't making much money. The army paid better than my brother did," continued Grant.

"Although you were in line to be a partner in the firm," said Sam, "And your one brother died of tuberculosis."

"Then there was the patriotism issue. All able-bodied men were supposed to work for the good of the country, and I had been educated at West Point."

"But everyone knew you were an alcoholic, Ulys. Initially the military didn't want you back. You kept trying, and finally you got back in, but maybe you could have served your country and your family just as well by staying in the leather business," said Sam.

"But it made my father happy, to see me go back into the army," said Grant.

Sam smiled, a sad, sympathetic smile. "So we're back to your father," he said.

Grant nodded, noticing that the ghosts were beginning to whirl around him again. A vision of Julia appeared, accompanied by a ghost who glowed with a silvery light. Julia was complaining that she was depressed living in a log cabin on the farm and asking if that was all there was to life. Grant could see and hear the silvery ghost telling Julia, "No, <u>this</u> is not your destiny. Cheer up, be happy now, and make the best of this. Up and be doing for your dear ones."

"And she did cheer up," Grant informed his angel. "She tried hard to make Hardscrabble look better, although I always knew that she wasn't happy with it. Maybe I wanted her to be proud of me, and being a military leader would do that, at least more so than working as a clerk for my brother at the store."

Grant appeared lost in thought as the sound of Julia's singing came back to him. "She always used to sing me a favorite ballad that declared 'the faithful soldier to be God's special care.' So being a soldier must be good, right?" he asked Sam.

"Well," said Sam, "The ballad was written by a human, so it would be tough to say. It could also refer to those who are working for God, soldiering on, shall we say, trying to live their life by God's commandments, to walk as closely to God's path as possible."

"You know, Julia told me that when she was ten or eleven years old, she was playing a game with her girlfriends, naming the occupations of their future husbands. And Julia said she told them she wanted 'a soldier, a gallant, brave, dashing soldier.' She always used to smile at me and say 'And I got one,' and hug my arm. That was how she saw me, as a gallant, brave, dashing soldier," said Grant.

"And compare this with how people perceived you when you returned home from California where you were stationed in 1854," said Sam. "Friends described you as 'dejected, low-spirited, badly-dressed and slovenly.' You were also drinking. How do you reconcile those two vastly different images of Ulysses as a soldier?"

"The Civil War was more interesting?" suggested Grant.

"Maybe, but you continued drinking off and on during that war too, although not as heavily as you had in your earlier days in the army," said Sam.

Just then the ghosts of two young soldiers appeared. It was the pair that Grant had ordered tied to a tree for leaving camp without authorization in search of 'seceshers.'

"We didn't do anything wrong, with all due respect, sir," said the taller of the two.

Grant nodded. "That's what the one minister said to me," he said to Sam. The two ghosts glared at Grant and floated off.

"It seems to me," said Sam, "That you felt that by taking the hard line about military rules, you could avoid the stickier issues, about life and death and such. You coped with the horrors of army duty by focusing on each activity as 'doing a good job.' That way, you didn't have to think about things like Cold Harbor, where you ordered the men into battle and lost 12,000 men's lives in fifteen minutes."

"That was a particularly bad example," said Grant. "What about Belmont? At Belmont, I prevented deaths," he asserted.

"You prevented deaths?" said Sam, his voice rising on the last syllable. "It is my understanding that Belmont was severely criticized in the North as a wholly unnecessary battle, barren of results."

"If it hadn't been fought, Colonel Oglesby would probably have been captured or destroyed with his 3,000 men. Then I should have been culpable indeed," said Grant, explaining his tactics. Tactics had always been his strong suit, other than horsemanship.

"But you were culpable," said Sam, slowly, in measured tones. "I can understand your point about

Colonel Oglesby, but <u>you</u> were responsible for the loss of 1127 men at Belmont."

"We only lost 485 men," said Grant, pondering the mathematics of the situation.

"On your side," said Sam, "And 642 Confederates. The battle was your idea, so you are morally responsible for the deaths and injuries of everyone on both sides. And 485 plus 642 equals 1127."

Grant nodded. "The math does indeed add up. But I hadn't looked at it that way. We only measure our casualties in terms of our own men, not the enemy side."

"But to God, the Creator, the lives of the Confederates are every bit as sacred and valuable as the lives of the Yankees. They are all children of the Same God."

Something stirred in the distant recesses of Grant's mind. "That sounds familiar, somehow," he said slowly, thinking. With a flash, the memory solidified.

"I know," said Grant. "One time when Julia was visiting me at camp, she was trying to give me advice about Vicksburg, and I told her that her suggestion would result in great loss of life and would not insure success. I even told her, 'This will all come out right in good time, and you must not forget that each and every one of my soldiers has a mother, wife or sweetheart, whose lives are as dear to them as mine is to you'."

To Grant's astonishment, Sam laughed. "I put that thought in your head," said Sam. "I was hoping that if you spoke it aloud to Julia, you would start to believe it yourself. You know, see one, do one, teach one. If you are teaching something to someone else, you are also learning it yourself."

Grant sighed and shook his head. "It sounded good, but you're right, it didn't sound like me--old 'Hit them hard and keep hitting' Captain Sam Grant. You were there with me. How come you didn't stop me?"

"I tried, many times," said Sam. "You weren't listening, and you weren't ready to listen and to under-stand. You preferred to stay focused on 'doing a good job.' People saw you as a man who was there at the behest of his country, a good citizen and loyal soldier. But to God's point of view, you were killing off thousands of His children. In four battles, you <u>lost</u> more men than Lee <u>had</u> in his whole army at the start of the war."

"So why didn't God stop me?" asked Grant. "Get me hit by a bullet like poor Hoskins, to whom I had loaned my horse."

"Because that would have been killing," replied Sam, "And God wouldn't do that to one of His children. He lets people make their own mistakes and then draw their own conclusions, since humans learn better by experience than by being told what to do. Even if He had said, 'Ulysses Grant, stop this killing at once and go home to your wife and children' would you have done it?"

"Certainly not," said Grant. "I wouldn't abandon my command, or go AWOL."

"So then how do you expect God to stop you?"

"Deliver a message?" asked Grant.

"Well, there was that time at Shiloh, where you got beyond the left of your troops," said Sam.

"And Colonel McPherson's horse was killed, struck by a bullet," said Grant, seeing the situation with clarity in his mind.

"Do you remember what happened to you?" asked Sam.

"A ball struck the metal scabbard of my sword and broke it nearly off," recollected Grant.

Sam nodded.

Grant looked at his mentor, realization slowly dawning on him. "That was you?"

Sam nodded. "I moved you out of the way, for you had so much to learn yet. I thought that a broken sword would clearly provide a message that you should stop fighting and go home. But you didn't take the hint." Sam looked sad.

The two spirits fell silent for a long while, each one lost in his own thoughts.

Sam broke the silence first. "How do you think these men felt in battle?"

"Loyal, especially before a battle. Scared, like I felt at that first battle, the one where Harris had already left," said Grant.

"What about pain? Do you think it hurts to get hit by a bullet? What about the emotional impact of shooting a gun at someone and seeing the bullet hit them, and knowing that you caused them pain and that they were now dying, never to eat another meal. Never again to dance with a girl. Never to go home to their parents, for a long awaited hug of reassurance. Never to walk the green earth again, nor splash in a creek. To have killed or to be killed. Both are painful."

"But they were troops," said Grant. "That was their job, just like mine was to lead them."

"These men were people. Remember, we are all children of the Same God. These 'troops' as you called them had wives, and children, and mothers and fathers and pets and farms, just as you pointed out to Julia but then promptly forgot what you had said. How would you have felt if someone walked up to you, point blank, and shot you, dead, the end?"

"Relieved," said Ulysses.

"Relieved?" asked Sam, seeking clarification.

"Yes, all my suffering in my life would be over, and I would have died a national hero," said Grant.

"That's really sad," said Sam. "To want your suffering to end in a violent way, rather than realizing that the part of you that contains a little bit of God could simply have changed his own path in life, could have left the army and started over somewhere. You could have re-created your own existence. And instead you thought it would be easier if you died." A concept was beginning to solidify in Sam's mind.

"So, what happened at Cold Harbor, when you ordered 12,000 men into battle and they were massacred in fifteen minutes?" asked Sam.

"I was drinking," confessed Grant. 'I know it was

wrong, I shouldn't have been drinking, me who used to give tirades against having alcohol in camp. But I was depressed."

"And you wished you were dead," said Sam. "So you ordered the men in your command into a situation where they were all slaughtered. Somehow you survived."

"And I felt terrible about it," said Grant.

"But you could have acknowledged you felt depressed about your life, and instead of that disaster at Cold Harbor, you could have taken sick leave and gone home for a while, until you felt better. You could have gone anywhere else, and chosen anything else, anything to have spared all those lives. All those innocent men and boys who trusted in their leader."

Just then, the ghost of a young soldier, about seventeen, in the blue uniform of the Union, came up to them. Looking directly at his commander, he said, "You didn't tell us we'd be slaughtered. I thought you would protect us. I thought we'd kill them Rebbies, not that they would kill us."

Grant looked keenly at the soldier. This boy was only a couple of years older than Grant's son Fred. The utter pathos of the situation struck him. Grant's big blue eyes misted over.

"What amazes me," said Sam, as the young soldier floated off, "Is that Cold Harbor wasn't the first time this happened. Let's start with Shiloh. You were responsible for 25,000 casualties."

"25,000?" asked Grant.

"Yes, 13,000 Union and 12,000 Confederate, roughly, since I don't have the specific numbers handy," said Sam. "People were shocked at these losses. They wanted you fired. They lobbied President Lincoln to get you removed. What happened?"

"I was drunk. Same thing as at Cold Harbor," admitted Grant.

"Plus, there was that whole fiasco with the dance hall girl, that was at Shiloh too," commented his guardian angel.

"I know," said Grant, sadly. "But I tried to not lose so many lives at Vicksburg. We only lost 9,362 to the Confederate 9,059."

"Only?" said Sam in an incredulous tone. "That's eighteen thousand four hundred and twenty-one people's lives! And you starved the town of Vicksburg."

"Well, it was better than killing them all," said

Grant.

"But remember, Thou Shalt Not Kill applies as much to one life as it does to a thousand. Each of those soldiers, on both sides, was a human being, a valuable child of God."

"I only lost 5,000 at Chattanooga," said Grant.

"To which I will give you the same reply. Five thousand deaths is five thousand too many."

"But what were we supposed to do? Let them secede? Destroy the Union that the founding fathers created?" asked Grant.

"But that's illogical," said Sam. "If we are protecting a document that says 'All men are created equal' but we think that we can kill some men in order to enforce that, then we are saying that all men are not equal, or you wouldn't have been able to perceive them as the enemy and to kill them. When all people are equal, no one can harm anyone else. We are all Children of the Sam God."

"Wait a minute," said Grant. "The Sam God?"

Sam smiled as he realized what he had said. "Sorry, must have been one of those Freudian slips I've heard about. I meant the Same God. Now, getting back to our topic, I will tell you the same thing about the Wilderness battles, where you were responsible for 17,000 casualties. They are all God's children, and there should have been no loss of life."

"Then how were we to solve the conflict?" demanded Grant. "War is a time-honored method of conflict resolution. It's what we learned at West Point. A good general is like an artist."

"An artist creates," said Sam. "A general destroys. And just because something is time-honored and has been around for a long time doesn't make it ethical or right. People made animal sacrifices to God for thousands of years, before Jesus came to teach that every life is sacred to God and God doesn't need to be worshiped by people killing God's creations and giving him dead carcasses of His creations."

"I never looked at it that way," said Grant. "But how were we to settle the conflict, if war and killing are wrong?"

"By discussion," said Sam, "As civilized people would do."

"But we were the pinnacle of Western Civilization. People looked up to us, and we became a world power by staying together as one country."

"But even if the other states had left, because of their philosophical disagreements, they may eventually have come back, in time," said Sam. "You have no way of knowing that. And war can be played out on a chessboard, or on the floor, with chalk and little pieces, and no one would get injured, and the same conclusions could be reached as those involving actual bloodshed. Philosophical issues related to governance shouldn't be resolved by seeing who kills more people. Kill or be killed is a terrible motivator to use as a decision factor in reaching an ethical decision. As God's children, we have an obligation to settle our conflicts peacefully, just as you would want your sons to settle a conflict. And just like any other children, if we don't know how to settle an argument, we need to ask our Father, the Father of all of us, the One True God. And if both sides had paid attention to God the Father, then there would have been no killing, and an equitable solution could have been reached. Sure, everyone may not have liked the decision, but that's how it is when siblings disagree. But the important thing is to follow the path that is closest to God, to follow His commandments."

"I know," said Grant. "And it's all such a muddle-

-duty to my parents, duty to my country, duty to the Academy, duty to my wife and children. My head feels like it is swimming."

"That's okay," said Sam. "Remember, I told you this would be a tough lesson, this one. But this was the biggest hurdle, and once we're over this one, you're more than halfway through all the lessons."

"But you were a warrior too," said Grant, thinking about some of the things that Sam had said. "How did you reconcile the things you had done with what you knew God wanted instead? You can't go back and undo the past."

"No," agreed Sam. "You can't undo the past. But you can learn from your mistakes, and you can do better in the future. And you can make amends to those you have wronged. And you can join in and help us work towards a better world, a world in which humans settle their differences with creative dialogue, not with weapons of destruction. A world where all people recognize that they are children of the same God, and they all work together for the common good. Where people consider the repercussions of their actions, and act out of love, rather than fear or anger."

"I'd like that, Sam," said Grant, earnestly. "I'd like to be a part of that kind of world, to not have to do things that I felt were wrong, like ordering troops into battle when I knew they'd be killed. My conscience has pained me so much all these years. Torn between winning the war for my country and my President, and the immense sorrow of all those lives lost. It was more than I could bear. That's part of why I kept drinking. And the ghosts--will they go away now?"

"Over time," said Sam. "As you work through these issues, and make amends, many of them will fade. Think of the ghosts as your friends, spirits that will help you on your way to this new and better world you will someday help to create. You can be a part of it, and from your greatest pain and anguish will come your greatest growth."

"And your pain went away?" asked Grant, still seeking reassurance.

"For the most part," said Sam. "But a part of it is always there. We can never truly be rid of things we have done, be they good or bad. They form a part of who we are. We have to own them, and take responsibility for them. So, since killing is wrong, it is best to live life with the resolution that from this point of awareness forward, you will not kill or cause anyone to be killed again."

"What about food? Humans are meat-eaters," said Grant.

"That is indeed a part of the issue," said Sam. "But as spirits evolve, they become less and less dependent on meat as a food source. They become aware of the fact that all living beings have feelings. Just as the Native Americans always thank the spirit of the animal who is providing them with food, all peoples of the earth need to understand this and to thank the spirit of the plant or animal for providing them with nourishment."

"Plants?" asked Grant.

Sam nodded. "Plants have feelings too. Lots of studies have shown that plants grow better when they are happy, when they are provided with a pleasant environment, and nice soft music, that sort of things. Have you ever thrown a log onto a fire and seen it weep, and heard a high-pitched screech-like noise?"

Grant nodded. "Several times I noticed that, especially when I was deep in thought and looking at the fire, thinking."

"That's from the spirit of the wood, and the tiny

creatures who have made their home in the log," said Sam. "There are millions of living organisms all around us, sharing the world with us, and people need to become more aware of these other living beings, to stop being so humanocentric, if such a word exists."

"Humanocentric," said Grant.

"Yes, centered on themselves, as if they are the only creature God made, the only thing important in the world. It's a dangerous point of view. It ignores all the other glorious and wonderful creations in God's world. And to get back to plants, yes they feel it when they are killed for food too. And man is an omnivore, someone who eats both plants and meat to survive. So the answer is to be kind in our food selection, to take only what is needed, and to take only food which has been raised for that purpose, since there the spirit of the animal or plant was able to choose that lifetime with the knowledge that its body would end up dying early to be used as food."

"What about fish?" asked Grant.

"If an organism is living free in the wild or the water, if you will, then it would be wrong to deprive that being of its freedom, and wrong to kill it for food. Humans are civilized enough to raise certain foods specifically for consumption, such as farm-raised catfish. There is no need to go out into the oceans and destroy the entire ocean culture by fishing and killing the plants and animals who live there. Whole habitats have been destroyed by humans in search of food, when there is plenty of other food available. There is no need to kill shrimp, or lobsters, or any other free being, for food. On the other hand, large cooperatives where chickens are raised purely for food, are another proposition. But we always need to grateful to the animal's spirit. You know lots of food that is fished or hunted is wasted, and people never eat it. They hunt, but won't eat what they killed, so therefore, they shouldn't hunt."

"So hunting is wrong?" asked Grant. "I never did like to hunt. I hated the idea of killing any thing, but my father thought this was foolishness on my part."

"Hunting is wrong," confirmed Sam. "Young Hiram Ulysses Grant was not being foolish, but wise, far wiser than his father. Your father just didn't have the sense to realize that he could learn from his child. There is no need for hunting and killing animals in the wild, destroying families. Humans forget that animals have families too. Just as a human family would be horrified if the father was shot and killed and some being ate it for food, it is the same feeling for a doe when her mate is shot, or any other wild animal for that matter. They have an entire world of their own that humans are unaware of, and so humans need to become more aware of these things, this other world, since this is all part of the vastness of God. God is a magnificent creator, who has created more things than we can even hope to imagine. And we need to start by becoming more aware of other creations with whom we share our space."

"Well, at least I knew that hunting was wrong," said Grant, with a faint smile. "Even if I didn't get the message at a larger scale. Then there was the whole issue of war and patriotism, and things like that."

"And someday, patriotism will mean sitting down to a discussion that lets us choose what is best for all people, within the structure of what God has taught us is right. To settle disputes fairly and equitably, showing kindness to all. To remember that no one <u>has</u> to win. When someone wins, someone else loses. And since all creatures are equally valuable in God's sight, there is no need for winners and losers. Personally, I can't even bear to watch the Olympics, that massive competition of athletes from all over the world. They are all excellent, and should just put on a pageant or show of their skills. They don't need to compete. What difference does it make in the grand scheme of things if one human can run a hundredth of a second faster around a track than another human? Early on, it may have conferred some sort of evolutionary advantage, but now the planet is packed. We don't need evolutionary advantage that way. All the athletes are good, and each and every one deserves a medal recognizing his achievements."

"Well," said Grant, "My head is still spinning, but I'll get over it. I just need some time to sift through all of this."

"You've got it," said Sam. "You want a day, a week, a month?"

"Two weeks," replied Grant. "That should give me enough time to think through all of this."

"Then two weeks it shall be," said Sam, with a twinkle in his eye. Grant was such a good pupil, thought Sam, hardworking and honest. Those were the qualities he liked best about his student, and he was glad that he had been chosen to be Grant's guardian spirit. "See you then."

And with that cheery note, Sam departed, and

Grant found himself sitting alone with his thoughts.

Chapter 10

Adultery

"Hey, Ulys, do you realize that in your book <u>The Personal Memoirs of U.S. Grant</u>, 54 of the 70 chapters are about the Civil War, and eleven chapters are about the Mexican War?" asked Sam one day.

Grant nodded. "Sounds about right to me, in terms of their importance."

Sam smiled to himself. *Got him here!* he thought. "You do realize that those were the parts of your life that Julia and the children didn't really share. You wrote little about the nearly 37 years of your marriage and family life, and nothing about your eight years in the White House. And yet, these are your _personal memoirs_, and as such would be expected to include things about your personal life. Otherwise, you might as well have called it the <u>Army Memoirs of U.S. Grant</u>."

"I did mention them. I know I discussed my marriage to Julia," commented Ulysses.

"Well, there's an entire page describing the town of Monterey, and by comparison, you dismiss your wedding to Julia with <u>one</u> <u>line</u>, two if you count your travels to your post at Sackett's Harbor, NY. And this was a wedding that Julia had dreamed about and planned for for four years of her life," said Sam.

"So what's your point, then?" asked Grant.

"Well, if we look at what you wrote as an index of its importance to you, then it would appear that the army was your first love. Granted, it was a love-hate kind of a relationship, that has left you with a lot of scars and ghosts, but if Julia was your wife, then the Army as such was your mistress, a mistress with such a great hold over you that it repeatedly drove you away from your wife and children, despite how much you feared combat and hated bloodshed."

"That's an interesting way of looking at it," acknowledged Grant.

"Of course, then there were the more traditional examples of adultery in your life, especially in the early days of your marriage. Like the summer of 1851, when you told Julia and little Fred to stay at White Haven, her parents' home, for the summer. In <u>September</u>, you wrote her a letter that she must come to see you, for you were anxious to see your little son. Julia wanted to believe that you wanted to see her also, but she was never quite certain you had mentioned wanting to see her."

Grant sighed. "Well, Fred was my first born son."

"But just because you had lots of other things to think about, doesn't mean that you weren't central in their thoughts. Then there was that whole episode in 1852, when you were ordered to California, and Julia was pregnant with your second son, Ulysses Jr., who was born July 22."

Grant marveled as always at his guardian spirit's fine command of the key dates and events in his life. *But then, I guess that's what guardian spirits do,* he thought.

Grant listened as Sam continued, "You decided Julia shouldn't go with you, since she was pregnant, and crossing Panama was difficult. You even told her that your salary was too small for them to have the common necessities of life out there, despite the fact that you were in charge of the division of married soldiers who had brought their families with them and all those other families managed to do well on their Army pay. Julia cried, and begged you to take them with, and while you told her to think about it overnight, you knew she would never do anything to displease you, and of course she stayed. She stayed, even though she knew about that little blond-haired wife of that one first lieutenant, and how she factored into your decision to leave Julia home."

"But that was just physical," said Sam.

"It was going on while your wife was pregnant, and would have continued out West if she hadn't been struck with cholera on the trip through Panama," said Sam.

"But Julia will never know," said Grant.

"Julia knew," said Sam. "She was very psychic, to use a current word, or fey, to use the Scottish word for it. Remember how she had that dream back when you were courting, that you would show up on a Monday, at noon, in civilian clothes, and that you would stay for a week?"

Grant nodded. "And it was just as she said."

Sam said, "Right. And there were many other times her dreams told her the truth. She suffered a lot, my friend, and she knew what was going on."

Grant felt a rising sense of panic. "I had no idea. What am I going to do?"

"Hang on," said Sam. "Julia is deceased too, remember. And she never said anything detrimental about you. A little ambitious on your behalf, but then so was your father; it's what you were used to. She did every-thing she could to defend and protect you, even writing indignantly in her own memoirs about those wretched Cincinnati newspapers that had reported that during the battle of Shiloh you were not in the field but were at a 'dance house'."

"She was a good wife," said Grant. "I didn't deserve her."

"Especially considering that the reports about the dance halls were true," said Sam. "Why else would a man who often commented that he couldn't and wouldn't dance be in a dance hall, paying women for their time?"

"But what about those times where I just flirted with them, just an innocent and harmless flirtation?" asked

Grant. "Lots of the soldiers did it; I wasn't the only one."

"It still doesn't make it right," replied Sam. "There is no such thing as an innocent flirtation, for there is sin in your heart even if not much occurred physically. It was still disloyal to your wife, who waited at home for you diligently and faithfully, naively trusting in you, despite what her intuition told her to the contrary. Thou Shalt Not Commit Adultery means being faithful to your spouse, in word, mind and deed. Not giving her any cause for suspicion. Not going to dance houses or houses of ill repute, like the ones out in California, or the ones in Mexico with the pretty senoritas."

"But what about my physical needs? What was I supposed to do about that?" demanded Grant.

"Let's see," said Sam. "You could have taken your wife with you wherever you went. You could have found another career and stayed home, where you and your wife could have had relations as often as you wanted. You had a number of options."

"But wasn't it better and safer for Julia to just stay home?" asked Grant.

Sam shook his head. "Only if you were at home as well. It isn't good for husbands and wives to be apart.

Like in the wedding ceremony, when the minister says 'What God has joined, let no man put asunder.' Marriage is about togetherness, and without that, there are far too many problems. God is so opposed to adultery that there are two commandments about it, the one we're discussing about not committing adultery, and the one about not coveting thy neighbor's wife. This is where the broader definition of infidelity comes from. Coveting and flirting are a form of infidelity because of the underlying desire to commit adultery."

Grant sighed, deeply chagrined. "If I'm lucky enough to ever find Julia in my next life, does this mean she's going to cheat on me to balance the scales?"

Sam replied, "Perhaps, if that's the only way that you can learn this lesson. But hopefully, you'll figure things out up here in the spiritual realm, and you'll be a much better spouse next lifetime. Besides, I don't think that's Julia's way. You just need to focus on how you would have felt if she had been carrying on with someone behind your back, how you would have felt if one of your children looked more like Robert E. Lee, who was a cousin of her good friend Mary, than he looked like you."

"She wouldn't!" declared Grant.

"True," said Sam, "but that's because she believed in God's commandment about not committing adultery, and she took her wedding vows seriously. And you can learn to do that too. By the way, you did do better in the later years of your marriage, at the White House and afterwards, and most people did perceive you and Julia as a devoted couple. But Julia's heart always ached with what she knew to be the truth."

"But she used to flirt with other men and dance with them, so I figured it was okay if I flirted with other women," said Grant.

"Just because she did something doesn't make it right. She has to answer for her own actions, too. But let's get back to your own actions," said Sam. "Like the time during the war when there was a problem with Pete Longstreet at Christmas, and Julia and the children were visiting you at camp. You left for Knoxville at early dawn the next morning and came home five days later, by way of a long visit in Lexington, Kentucky. Then you actually had the temerity to tell Julia of the many pretty young ladies you had met there and how much you had enjoyed yourself during that visit! And all the while, your wife and children were back at camp, waiting for you, enjoying a lonely Christmas, while you were having fun with a bunch of Kentucky belles. What do you make of that?"

"But she didn't complain or yell at me," pointed out Grant.

"Because she believed that you were doing what you needed to on behalf of the country. But your duty to the country did not involve committing adultery on Christmas. That is preposterous, if I do say so myself. And, as I've often said, it really wouldn't have mattered if you'd let the whole Longstreet thing slide, since he was Julia's cousin. He wasn't going to do you much harm, since if he killed Julia's husband he wouldn't have been able to forgive himself for bringing her such unhappiness. While you may not have been in love with her, she was in love with you."

"She was in love with her idea of who I was," said Grant.

"True," said Sam, "but that still doesn't make your behavior right. By any standards, that Christmas fiasco was less than honorable behavior. And yes, Julia should have yelled at you and carried on, but she wasn't brought up to do that. Her mother silently endured such behavior from her father, without complaining. Many wives of famous men put up with poor behavior by their spouse, for a variety of reasons, including not wanting to rock the boat, that they loved the man in question, that they regarded it as flattering that other women were interested in their man, since that made the man seem more desirable, and the list could go on and on."

"Well, they shouldn't put up with it," said Grant. "And then it would have to stop."

"Especially because Julia was jealous. Like all the women that would come to you and want a button off your coat for a souvenir. She resented all of them, and one time she did tell you how she felt; after that you decided to send the women to Julia to ask for a button."

"And Julia still gave them one anyhow," said Grant.

"But she resented it tremendously," said Sam. "She thought it was her duty, though, as the wife of a famous general."

"So she had her own issues," said Grant.

"True," agreed Sam. "And we're here to work on your issues, and only those of hers as impact on you and your life and the choices you made."

"Be that as it may, it's time for me to go now,"

said Sam. "I'll see you tomorrow." And Sam floated off, leaving behind a sense of darkness.

Grant looked forward to seeing his mentor again the following day, wondering how he too could become a part of the light and warmth that characterized his very wise teacher.

"So," said Sam. "Today we'll talk about the eighth commandment. Do you recall that one?"

Grant struggled. "We've covered that there is only One God and discussed the concept of false gods. We've talked about graven images and respect for that which is holy. We've talked about God's name and using it appropriately. Honoring thy parents was a big one, and we just finished discussing the whole adultery issue. Hmm, I guess stealing and lying and coveting are left."

"Right," said Sam. "God's eighth commandment

says 'Thou Shalt Not Steal'."

"But I don't steal," said Grant. "At least not in the conventional sense of the word. Well, I did take all our money in the first years of our marriage and squander it on dance halls and alcohol and gambling, and that was taking money away from Julia and the children."

Sam nodded as he thought about how Grant's honesty was one of his endearing qualities.

"So a broader definition for our purpose would be Thou Shalt Not Take Anything That Is Not Yours To Take," said Sam.

Grant nodded. "That sounds clearer."

"Okay," said Sam. "Let's talk about the time you were the regimental quartermaster in the Mexican war and responsible for the procurement of horses."

Grant took a deep breath as if he could smell the horse manure even now. "Ah horses," he said. "Those Mexican mules were the stubbornest things I've ever seen. I wouldn't wish them on my worst enemy."

"And how did you get those horses?" asked Sam.

"Bought them from the Mexican traders for $36 a dozen," replied Grant, not seeing how this was relevant to the present topic.

"And where did the Mexican traders get the horses?" pressed Sam, as if he were leading a child.

"They were wild. There were hundreds of them on the loose. The Mexicans would round them up and we'd brand them with the U.S. brand and teach them to pull the wagons. Stubborn things," said Grant.

"So let's get this straight," said Sam. "You and the Mexicans cooperated together to capture wild horses and mules and brand them and force them to pull wagons and you complain that they were stubborn because they didn't want to do what you wanted them to do. Did it ever occur to you that what you were doing was cruel and mean?"

"But we needed to carry the supplies on wagons," said Grant.

"And what would have happened if there were no wild horses and no Mexican traders?" asked Sam.

"We'd have had to procure some from up north or have headquarters send some down," said Grant, not seeing where this might be leading.

"Or you could have done without them," said Sam.

Grant denied that this could have occurred.

"Where did you all lose the idea that animals are living beings, that they are God's creatures as surely as humans are? They feel pain; they resent losing their freedom. When Africans herded up bunches of their own people and put them in shackles and packed them onto boats and sold them to dealers in the United States and other places, that was 'slavery' and regarded as so wrong by the North that a war was fought to abolish it. IN WHAT WAY is capturing a wild horse, who lives free on the plains, and tying him with rope and branding him with a searing hot iron and harnessing him, to lead a life of servitude, any different? You enslaved these animals, you and the Mexicans, and others who have done the same thing. Who are you, or any human, to decide this for any of God's creatures?" Sam was indignant.

"But the Bible says man has dominion over all the animals," said Grant.

"And a human wrote the Bible," replied Grant. "For all you know, the hornets could have a Bible that says the hornets have dominion over all creatures and they can 'prove it' because they can sting."

Grant laughed.

"This is serious," said Sam. "This is one of the

biggest misconceptions that humans have, that they have dominion. <u>To God alone belongs dominion</u>, and all of God's creatures need to exist together in harmony, respecting the rights of each other and doing no harm to each other. No one creature that God created is any 'greater' than any other. Each is special and unique in his or her own way, like snowflakes."

"But what about bugs, like ants," said Grant, thinking of the most ludicrous example he could, to show that man really was superior.

"What about them? Who is to say that their societal organization is not superior to that of humans? Ants have had a well-organized society that is older than that of humans. They are hard-working, and have a clear division of labor. They are very advanced, if you take time to study them. They can accomplish a lot by working slow and steady, which is a favorite theory of yours, but one which they apply to peaceful activities such as building homes for their families. There are just as many ants in the world as humans, if not more. Parallel societies, co-existing in time, and yet humans don't think about them because of the size differential. But if both humans and ants were the same size, then a fairer comparison could be made."

Grant sighed. "I see what you mean. So the horses weren't ours to take, any more than slaves were. And just because someone else enslaves someone or something, we don't have to perpetuate it by buying the item."

"Right," said Sam. "You're getting the idea. Like tropical birds who are captured and sold for pets. Millions of them die in the process of being captured and then exported from their homes. If people would stop buying them, there would be no reason for unscrupulous traders to capture these beautiful animals in order to sell them. Supply and demand are like that; if you get rid of demand, there is no need for supply. And we'd get to a healthier level of respecting all of God's creations."

"So are all horses wrongly enslaved?" asked Grant. "I was such a good horseman. First in my class at West Point in horsemanship. I even set a record by jumping my stallion higher than any horse had ever jumped there."

Sam stifled a laugh. "Now, Ulys, do you think the horse enjoyed that?"

"No, but I sure did," said Grant.

"And then there was your use of spurs. Would you like someone to kick you in a vulnerable spot with metal spikes in order to make you move?"

"But everyone used them," protested Grant.

"That doesn't make it right," said Sam. "As your mother would have said, If everyone jumps off a bridge, it doesn't mean you should too. A truly good horseman, who works with animals the way God intends, uses only his voice and a soothing touch to achieve the animal's cooperation, and respects the animal's rights to decide what he or she will or will not do, with all choices being okay with the person. You can't control another being, no matter what all that military training taught you. There are always consequences to controlling others or trying to. So, having a horse if it has been born a domesticated horse is not necessarily wrong. But you need to treat the horse with the recognition that his spirit and being are equal to yours in the eyes of the Creator, and to be aware of his feelings. For instance, if you have two horses and they have children, don't divide up the family and sell off the children for profit or give them away. You wouldn't have wanted someone to do that to your children, right? Some other species to say, Hey, Grant and his wife have four kids and they only need one, so let's take their other three and sell them, and the Grants will never see them again."

"Whew," said Grant. "That really is mean, when I look at it that way. And millions of farmers and pet owners do exactly that every day."

"And come back as animals or slaves somewhere in the world so that they can learn that what they did was wrong," said Sam. "Remember, all actions have consequences."

Grant shook his head to clear away the vivid image of another species selling off what it perceived as Grant's unnecessary extra children. It had brought the horrors of slavery home to him in a way that nothing during his lifetime had. Taking those horses had been wrong, too. Ulysses could see in his mind the horses running free over the plains, their hair flying in the wind, enjoying their freedom. And then humans had enslaved them, stolen away from them that delicious freedom of riding free, and destroying the horses' family structure. Life was really unfair to these creatures, and Grant had played a part in that. He was overwhelmed with his own responsibility in this crime against the noblest of all animals, at least in his humble opinion. He hung his head, and was so lost in his thoughts that he never even noticed

Sam's departure that day.

"Let's see if I understand this whole Jewish episode," said Sam one day. "Back on December 17, 1862, you issued an order called 'General Orders Number Eleven' which read as follows:

I. The Jews, as a class, violating every regulation of trade established by the Treasury Department, and also Department orders, are hereby expelled from the Department. II. Within twenty-four hours from the receipt of this order by Post Commanders, they will see that all of this class of people are furnished with passes and required to leave, and any one returning after such notification, will be arrested and held in confinement until an opportunity occurs of sending them out as prisoners unless furnished with permits from these Head Quarters (sic). III. No permits will be given for these people to visit Head Quarters for the purpose of making personal application for trade permits."

"And what of it?" said Grant. "Everyone knows the Jews are only out to make money."

"Everyone knows this?" asked Sam. "The religious hero that you all worship, Jesus, was a Jew. He advocated giving up all one's worldly goods and living communally. I've never met a man less concerned with money and worldly things. He always felt that his Father would provide for all of his needs."

"Jesus was a Jew? Are you sure?" asked Grant.

"Of course I'm sure," replied Sam. "He visits all of us occasionally to see if anyone wants or needs his help. He's a great guy."

"But that doesn't prove he was Jewish," argued Grant.

"Well, his mother was Jewish, and his father was Jewish. All his siblings were Jewish. He had a traditional

Jewish upbringing, complete with Bar Mitzvah at age thirteen, the Jewish ceremony of becoming an adult in the Jewish faith. Remember when he got lost from his parents in Jerusalem that time and was arguing with the religious leaders?"

Grant nodded.

"They were Jewish rabbis. In fact, Jesus became a rabbi, a teacher. He sought to make some changes in Judaism that would make the faith more accessible to all people, not just the wealthy. Jesus taught that all people are equal in the sight of God, and invited all to join him at his table. He ate with people like Matthew the tax-collector, who was considered 'unclean' and not welcome at the tables of the righteous. Just because a person wasn't well-educated didn't make them 'unclean,' Jesus argued."

"So where did Christianity come from, then?" asked Grant.

"The word Christ apparently came from the word for Messiah, which many applied to Jesus. He himself never claimed to be the Messiah. He said he was the Son of Man, as we all are, when we realize that God created each of us and that our goal is to walk as close to the path of God as possible," said Sam. "After his death, Saul, who had previously been persecuting the followers of Jesus and stoning them to death in the streets had a vision in which God asked him why he was doing this. Saul realized that what he had been doing was wrong, recanted, and vowed that he would work on the team of Jesus' followers. Only, as I understand it, that wasn't glamorous enough for Saul, and he called these followers Christians and created the concept of the new religion he called 'Christianity.' Much of the New Testament is work by and about Saul, who took the name Paul after his 'seeing the light' and 'changing teams' so to speak. If we discard from the New Testament all of the work by Paul, and I'm not necessarily saying we need to do that, but I'll discuss that in a minute, then what we have is a biography of a gifted follower of God, who taught two fundamental truths: Love One Another as I Have Loved You, and There is One God, which is based on the Jewish prayer called the sh'ma."

Grant listened intently. Religion as preached in the churches he had attended had never mentioned any of this, and yet it all rang true. Not to mention that it was much more interesting than the fire and brimstone preaching he had heard in church, with its threats of damnation if a person didn't do as the <u>church</u> wanted, such as to make certain contributions.

"So what about removing Paul's stuff from the Bible?" prompted Grant.

"Well, for starters, a lot of the people known as 'fundamentalists' would regard this as heresy, because they believe that every word of the Bible is literally true."

"And it isn't?" asked Grant.

"No," said Sam, shaking his head. "It's a book of stories, an oral legend that was never to be written down. Alas, some scholarly rabbi way back before Jesus decided to make it his life's work to write it down, and that's what he did. There were several different versions of lots of the stories, and people often forget to factor in the human element of the storyteller, our personal biases that affect anything that we write. Try it sometime--see if you can write a story that is completely bias-free. It's very tough to do. So, to get back to the writings of Saul/Paul, what needs to be taught is that Paul was a person, a human being with his own issues to deal with. He tried to bring Jesus' teachings to the 'gentiles' or non-Jews, without them understanding Judaism, which is the foundation that underlies all of Jesus' teachings, and underlies his very existence in fact. In this way, Paul did a huge disservice to all of mankind, especially those who believe everything Paul ever said or wrote to be 'the gospel truth.' When Jesus said, 'The way to the Father is through me,' he meant that we should understand God through living a life like Jesus', understanding the Jewish roots that were the foundation of his beliefs, and walking as close to God's path as possible. Jesus wasn't saying to worship Jesus as a god, which would be a false god, for Jesus as a son of God was basically a messenger. God has sent many of these messengers over the course of history, and some-times people understand a little of the message, and sometimes they miss it. In the worse case scenario, such as Jesus', the townspeople and the authorities killed the messenger."

"Fascinating," said Grant. "I never looked at it this way. It's all so _human_."

"And that's why God sends these messengers," said Sam. "To make the message more human. But humans are a stubborn lot, and as best as I can tell, they only learn the message when they are ready to learn it. Otherwise their own self-serving ambitions get in the way."

"Like I said about the Jews," said Grant.

"No," said Sam. "It's true of people of all nations, all races, all colors and religions, although of the people I've met, the Buddhists seem to do a bit better at getting past self-serving ambition, and looking for the inner meaning of things. By the way, did you know that Jesus studied the Eastern religions?"

"You're kidding, right?" said Grant.

"No, I'm quite serious. There are signs in India of places he visited. We're spirits; we can go there if you'd like. He apparently studied the Eastern religions during those years from fourteen to twenty-eight or so where there is not much written record of his life."

"Maybe Paul destroyed those records because they didn't fit in with his views," suggested Grant.

"Could be," agreed Sam. "So, to get back to this order you issued in the military, no one has ever comprehended this action. Your wife Julia disliked what she called 'that obnoxious order.' In fact, you lost the highest ranking Jewish officer in your command, Lt. Colonel Marcus M. Spiegel, 120th Ohio, the son of a German rabbi, who was with his regiment on Sherman's expedition to Vicksburg at the time. Furthermore, there were roughly *ten thousand* Jewish soldiers in the Civil War, on the sides of both North and South. Their religion had mixed views about slavery."

"Weren't they once slaves in Egypt?" asked Grant, thinking about Bible history.

"True," said Sam. "So you'd think that would make them vehemently opposed to slavery. But if we look closely at the Bible story of this, some wanted to leave Egypt with Moses, and many were afraid. They preferred their life as slaves for the simple reason that it was what they were used to. They knew they would have food, and if abuse came with the deal, that's what they were used to. The unknown felt very scary to them. Many of them wanted to turn back. That's why God kept them out in the desert so long, until that group died off and the young ones weren't attached to the concept of slavery as security. The group couldn't move on until they put that concept behind them, for slavery goes against God's teaching that all people are equal in His sight."

Grant nodded. "Got to get the troops in order before you can proceed."

"Exactly," said Sam. "I've seen the same thing in a number of people here who were more comfortable with the abuser rather than taking a chance on the unknown in their most recent life."

"So the victims of abuse are here?"

"Like Gregorio, yes. There are always choices, like running away, like those slaves that created and utilized the Underground Railroad did," said Sam.

"But a lot of them got killed trying to escape," said Grant.

"Right, they did. But once they had gotten to the point that their life just wasn't worth living, then they considered other choices. Some tried to kill their masters. Some, who didn't believe in killing, fled. Had all the slaves united, they would have been a fearsome force."

"So what kept them slaves?" asked Grant. "I know the ones at Julia's father's place, White Haven, had it pretty good, with plenty of food and places to live."

"But they didn't have their freedom. And freedom is a precious gift. God doesn't mean for any of us to be slaves," said Sam. "He gives us the ability to make choices in our life, to choose our path, to choose right from wrong. Take you for instance. You were a slave to your father's ambitions, and then your wife's ambitions. As you said earlier, you never did get to do what Hiram Ulysses Grant really wanted to do. And you felt that incredible rush of happiness at the thought of being _free_ to be whatever you wanted. So, in your next life, that will probably be a key issue for you."

Sam took a deep breath and stretched. "Ah, but we've digressed quite a bit. So, let's take a break, and we'll discuss that General Orders Number Eleven tomorrow, after you've had a chance to think about what we've talked about today."

Grant agreed. It had been a long and thought-provoking discussion. After Sam left, Grant sat and thought for quite a while, and eventually drifted off to sleep.

The chair. Grant was sitting in <u>that</u> chair, the homemade one with the rough wood where he could see and feel the grains of the wood, in the dream. Must be a dream, since he wasn't wearing shoes, which must mean he was dead. His arms rested so comfortably in that chair. It had been made especially for him, at Chattanooga. It was like an old friend. He had just finished writing a letter, a reply to one of Julia's letters, in which she interceded on behalf of her friend Mary for a favor. "She took a risk in writing that to me," thought Grant. "But she means well, my Julia." He had written the letter she had requested, after a lengthy debate about the ethics of it, but he could see Julia's point, since this was Julia's cousin to whom he was writing. At that point, Rawlins came in, and Grant had hidden what he was writing from view. Drat that Rawlins. He was always watching over me like a mother hen. But Rawlins would have been aghast at the letter Julia had asked her husband to send, and after Rawlins had left Grant's tent, Grant had hidden the letter under the chair, deep under the seat where the seat met one of the two pieces of wood that formed the legs of the chair. He had then written another letter as a decoy, and sent the bland decoy to Julia instead.

Grant could see Rawlins in the dream, reading the ersatz letter, shaking his head in wonder as to why Grant had thought it necessary to hide this, for although it was a bit whiny about how much he missed Julia, there was nothing that unusual about that. Lots of the men in the regiment missed their wives. It was part of being a soldier, thought Rawlins, as he placed the letter in the post bag.

Grant woke up. Now where was that letter? he

wondered. If only he could have seen more in the dream. Maybe it was a clue of some sort. He tried to fall back to sleep to recapture the dream, but with no success.

A long while later, Sam returned. Grant sighed. Today's the day we're going to discuss that order about the Jews. Where to even begin? wondered Grant.

Sam had been wondering the same thing. But through dogged persistence, he would get to the bottom of this.

Grant spoke first. "It wasn't my fault. It was the whole cotton trade thing."

Sam listened patiently.

"Back in February 1862, my victory at Fort Donelson, Tennessee, cracked the Confederate defense line in Tennessee and opened part of the cotton kingdom to Federal occupation," said Grant, in his best military style. "The outbreak of war had so greatly increased the value of cotton in the North and in Europe that the Southern planters continued to grow it, despite the embargo and Union blockade."

"However, there were a number of loopholes in the government policy on trade," continued Grant. "When the war first began, Secretary of the Treasury Salmon P. Chase moved immediately to stop the shipping of 'munitions of war' to the Confederate states. It wasn't until August of 1861 that President Lincoln gave the Treasury the authority to regulate trade with insurrectionary regions. As armies moved southward, Treasury agents gave permits to loyal citizens to resume normal commerce, since Chase believed that trade should follow the flag. Chase apparently thought that such a policy would reconcile citizens with the Federal government and benefit the Northern economy by the flow of needed Southern products."

"From the Army perspective, this whole trade thing was one big nightmare, since goods traded by so called 'loyal persons' somehow seeped southward to the Confederacy in exchange for cotton. The government had expected that any captured cotton would be sold to benefit our Treasury and defray the costs of the war. But as the army advanced, the secesh burned their cotton rather than see it go to the North. Rebels who were aware that we were coming and who were reluctant to burn their only capital asset had an alternative, and would trade the cotton with traders or their agents for gold, weapons or medicine.

The speculators who bought the cotton this way stood to make enough profit that they could bribe the officers and officials to look the other way or even to assist in the smuggling of the cotton through the lines. Can you believe it? I mean, do you blame me for trying to stop this whole fiasco?" asked Grant.

"But wasn't your father Jesse involved in this whole cotton trading business?" enquired Sam, ever so politely, for he already knew that that had been the case.

Grant sighed. No point lying, since Sam was his spirit guide, the one sent to help him sort things out. "Yes," he confessed, "My father had just arrived in Mississippi to buy cotton for a Jewish firm in Cincinnati in exchange for one quarter of the profits."

"Ah, yes, your father," said Sam. "One of his neighbors once described Jesse R. Grant as being 'willing to follow a dollar to hell.' And yet he always claimed to be such a patriotic and a religious man. Your father; we could spend hours discussing him, but let's get back to this cotton matter. Do you suppose that it was easier to direct your anger against the Jews, since there was a prevailing undercurrent of anti-Semitism anyhow, rather than express anger at your father, who in your perception was subverting your efforts to win the war on behalf of the Union."

"But the Jews are always in business," said Grant.

Sam shook his head. "There was an investigation in 1863 of cotton-buying in the Mississippi Valley. It involved hundreds of soldiers and civilians, and how many of them do you think were Jewish?" asked Sam.

"Three fourths of them, at least," replied Grant.

"No," said Sam. "Out of all those hundreds, only four people involved were Jewish. Which would make your accusations false."

"But it was only that once," said Grant.

"I don't think so," said Sam. "On July 26, 1862, you telegraphed your subordinate in Columbus, Kentucky, from Corinth, Mississippi. You said, and I quote, 'Examine the baggage of all speculators coming South, and when they have specie, turn them back. If medicine and other contraband articles, arrest them and confiscate the contraband articles. Jews should receive special attention'."

"Do you remember that?" Sam asked.

Grant acknowledged that he did with a nod of his head.

"Then, as if that wasn't enough, on November 9 you telegraphed Major General Stephen A. Hurlbut at

Memphis and said, 'Refuse all permits to come south of Jackson for the present. The Israelites especially should be kept out.' The next day, you instructed your superintendent of military railroads to 'Give orders to all the conductors...on the road that no Jews are to be permitted to travel on the Rail Road southward from any point. They may go north and be encouraged in it but they are such an intolerable nuisance. That the Department must be purged for them.' I just don't see this as a one-time statement on your part," said Sam. "There's so much anti-Jewish sentiment that you expressed. I could go on with several more examples, since you left quite a paper trail."

"Well," said Grant, "At my inaugural address in 1869, I did say that I know of no method to secure the repeal of bad or obnoxious laws so effective as their stringent execution."

"So, in that mean-spirited tone," said Sam, "Your orders were carried out in Paducah, Kentucky, for instance, where all the Jews were expelled on twenty-four hour notice. Entire families were driven from their homes, including the two old army veterans you've seen as ghosts. How would you have felt if this had been done to you? If you and Julia and your children were driven from your home, on the whim of someone who had decided to do this just because you were, say, white? Would that be fair?"

"No one would do that to whites," said Grant.

Sam raised his eyebrows. "The color of a person's skin shouldn't matter. In the healthiest of worlds, we will all be neutral about color, since God created humans in all different shades, and we are all created in His, or Her, image. God is greater than color or gender or creed, and transcends any limiting factor. So, for the sake of argument, let's say you and your family are driven out of your home by hostile people on a pretext you know is false. How would you feel?"

"I don't know," said Grant.

"Think. Let's think about one of your earliest lessons, the Golden Rule. Do Unto Others as You Would Have Them Do Unto You. Do you think that your actions displacing these people were fair?"

"I was trying to win the war for the North," persisted Grant.

"But the Jews weren't responsible for the cotton trade," said Sam. "They were falsely persecuted and harmed, at your direction. How do you propose to make amends for this?"

"Do I have to?" asked Grant.

"Well, let's consider your options," said Sam. "God clearly states 'Thou Shalt Not Bear False Witness.' You clearly bore false witness. Now, the first order of business would be to admit that you made a mistake, and then you need to make amends. This is a big insult to the people God refers to as His 'Chosen People.' Jesus, as you will recall from our discussion yesterday, was Jewish. The Old Testament is Jewish. Personally, I don't think you can insult a large group of people with impunity. But, since you don't seem ready to deal with this, we can 'put it on the back burner,' so to speak. Sometimes, we make rapid progress in dealing with our issues, and sometimes we hit things that are stumbling blocks. Maybe this one is so tough for you because your father's partners were Jewish, and you don't want to look at the issues about your father. So, suffice it to say, I've discussed my part of this commandment, and the rest is up to you."

"So that's it?" asked Grant. "You're not going to make me apologize to the Jews?"

"Not if you don't want to," said Sam. "Remember, Im only your spirit helper, your guide. I'm not God. It's up to you and Him to decide how you will learn certain experiences that you aren't willing to work on. When you are ready to move ahead, the right teacher or setting for your growth in that area will occur. Whether you will choose to be born as a Jew, or to learn all you can about the Jews, or to apologize will be up to you. But always remember that there are fundamental truths in life, such as the one that all people are created equal. Anytime you forget part of this, you will have to relearn the truth. The pace is up to you."

"That's a pretty fair deal," said Grant.

"I know," smiled Sam. "We practice unconditional acceptance, accepting each person just as they are, with their good points and their flaws. We try really hard not to judge, although it isn't always easy, and we're always learning and improving."

"Who are the 'we'?" asked Grant.

"Me, the other angels and spirit helpers and teachers and guides, the council that helps you choose your next lifetime so you will learn the lesson you are ready to learn, and of course God," replied Sam.

"Oh," said Grant.

"So, on that note, I think we've discussed the ninth commandment enough for now, and I shall leave you to your rest. See you later," said Sam as he drifted off into the ether.

Chapter 13

Coveting

Grant and his angel Sam were sitting around one day, observing the great-great grandson of John Rawlins, a Timothy P. Rawlins, to be precise. Timothy, or Tim as the young man was known, had inherited his ancestor's dark good looks, and a love of horses from his mother's side of the family. Young Tim had grown up here in Virginia, on a horse farm of several hundred acres.

"They've done quite well without slaves," commented Grant. "You know, Rawlins met his wife Mary Emma when we were stationed in the South. She was a governess for one of the secesh families, the Lums, at one of the houses where we stayed. The family always sent her down to ask for favors, such as the use of a horse so that the family could go to market, that sort of thing, since she was a very attractive girl. Next thing I knew, Rawlins was marrying her."

"So he married a Southern girl?" asked Sam.

"No," said Grant. "To be honest, she was originally from Connecticut. I'm not quite sure what she was doing working for a secesh family. Anyhow, after the war, somehow they ended up back in the South, and one of their children married into a wealthy Virginia family, and the results are what we see here."

Grant sighed deeply. "I wish my life had been that easy. To meet the right person, and get married just like that. To have plenty of money, a glorious farm, not like Hardscrabble, that I built with my hands. It was the best I could do, though," said Grant. "But Julia never liked it. She always wanted something more elegant. I think the only years she was really happy were when we lived in the White House and then afterwards, when we traveled around the world and were entertained and greeted with enthusiasm wherever we went."

Grant looked at the horse Tim was riding and sighed again. "What a glorious horse. Oh to be human again. To feel the power of the horse under the saddle. To become one with the horse as we jumped over a fence in a sun-drenched pasture."

Sam looked at Ulysses. "Coveting, hunh?"

"What do you mean?" asked Grant.

"Wanting something that belongs to someone else, or wanting something we don't have or can't have," replied Sam.

"Is it one of the commandments?" asked Grant, smiling. "We're due for another lesson, I know."

Sam chuckled. "Yes, it is. It's the tenth commandment, and it says 'Thou shalt not covet thy neighbor's house; thou shalt not covet thy neighbor's wife, or his manservant, or his maidservant, or his ox, or his ass, or anything that is thy neighbor's'."

"Guilty as charged," said Grant. "I've coveted other people's horses for as long as I can remember. Back when I was fifteen, I was visiting some friends of the family, and they had this saddle horse I decided I wanted, and so I traded the horse I had ridden over there for it. The man whose house and horse it was said he felt strange trading with a mere youth, but my friend assured him that I had permission to do such things. He even gave me some money as well, to even out the trade."

Grant chuckled suddenly as Sam watched him with interest.

"So what happened then?" asked Sam.

"The horse was so skittish that I had to put a blindfold on him to even get to my uncle's house in Maysville, where I borrowed a better horse from my uncle in order to make it home."

"What did your parents say?" asked Sam.

"They saw how chagrined I was at having to borrow a horse from my uncle to make it home, and my father went with me back to the man I had traded with to get our horse back," said Grant. "You think I would have learned after that, but I kept coveting horses, trading for them, buying them, for years. Even now, I yearn to be back in the saddle on a horse. It was my best subject at West Point, you know, when they got a riding instructor and he used to let me help break in the new horses. It made being there at the Academy more tolerable. Before that, I used to keep hoping that Congress would pass a bill abolishing the Academy so that I would have an honorable way out, but no such luck."

"So," hypothesized Sam, "Do you suppose that coveting might serve a useful educational function? Setting aside the matter of whether coveting is right or wrong, for the sake of discussion, of course."

"Well," considered Grant, "Coveting horses brought me my share of trouble, but it also taught me how to deal with people. How to beware of something that looked like a bargain but wasn't."

"Ulyss, Ulyss, you really think you learned that one? You got swindled twice while you were stationed out in California, years after the horse incident. You lost $1500 to a merchant of a general store who enticed you to be a partner in his store in exchange for the money, and $2000 to the husband of that blonde woman, Helen, who had opened a banking business. When you were ready to head home in 1854, you had to delay the trip by two weeks to try to get your money back from the banker, who claimed he needed two weeks to get the money. The banker, Helen's husband, disappeared, and you had to depend on the quartermaster for transportation to New York. Years later, Julia wrote to the man, asking for the money which had been owed to you since 1854."

Grant nodded. "Sherman offered to lend me the money, but I didn't want to bother him with my problems. Besides, if it hadn't been for Helen, I wouldn't have been involved in the whole banking thing with her husband, and I certainly couldn't tell Sherman the whole sordid tale. He'd have thought I was an idiot, or worse."

"Of course, it was customary for the steamship company to give all officers on leave for home free passage back then," said Sam. "But you didn't take advantage of that offer."

"No," sighed Grant. "I used most of the money from the quartermaster for alcohol, and I wasn't thinking too clearly. Going via the steamship offer, where I would have paid only for my meals, would have been the way to go."

"Isn't it amazing that a fellow such as yourself who was so good at mathematics all through school, and yearned to be a professor of mathematics, was so bad with money?"

"Money," said Grant. "When I was paymaster, I used to look at the paltry amount the soldiers were getting, and I couldn't figure out how they managed on that little bit of money. In fact, that's what I was thinking about and doing the day I was drunk on duty, when my superior said he was going to court-martial me. I resigned shortly thereafter. Of course, for years later, people referred to me as Sam Grant, the drunk. That reputation didn't really leave me until President Lincoln said that if I was drinking, he'd like to know what I drank so he could give it to the other generals as well."

"But you never handled money well," said Sam. "You lost your farm; every business venture you went into ended disastrously. After the 1880 Republican convention, you dabbled in business and moved to New York City to become a silent partner in your son Ulysses Jr.'s firm, Grant and Ward."

"How were we to know that Ferdinand Ward was a swindler?" asked Grant. "He was my son's business partner."

"Caution is always a good idea," suggested Sam. "Keep most of your money in a conservative format, and only risk that which you could afford to lose. If you hadn't written your memoirs in your final year of life, your wife would have been destitute, penniless."

"Hmmm," said Grant. "Do you think maybe I was so bad with money so that I could punish myself and others?"

"Could be," said Sam. "You knew what had happened with Helen was wrong, so you got involved with her husband in his banking business. You lost your hard-earned money and were penniless, and figured it was what you deserved. Of course, it hurt Julia and your children as well."

"And why would I have wanted to lose all the money in my later years?" asked Grant.

"I think you felt a sense of sadness, of loss, that you had never gotten to live the life you had wanted. Nothing you enjoyed was ever good enough for Julia, and reducing this daughter of wealth and privilege who was from one of St. Louis' finest families to being penniless was a way of getting back at her."

Grant considered this a moment, stroking his beard as he thought. "You know, I believe you are right. It all makes sense. Here I built her a beautiful cabin, all with the labor of my own hands, and she named it Hard-scrabble because the cabin seemed so rough and homely to her. She kept moaning about how she was trying to fix it up and make it nice for us, but she just couldn't do much with it. She never seemed to understand how that made me feel. I mean, I wasn't all that sold on the whole idea of marriage anyhow, but I stuck it out, and I stayed by her, and even spent eight years in the White House so she'd be proud of me."

"I know," said Sam, sympathetically. "I figured it wasn't a marriage based on romance on your side when you wrote that in May of 1844 you and 'the young lady came to an understanding that at a convenient time we would join our fortunes.' And later you wrote, on August 22, 1848, that you had 'fulfilled this agreement.' Hardly the most romantic of terms to described a much awaited betrothal and marriage. And especially considering that you used to read all sorts of novels, especially romances. So I'm sure you knew the romantic words. And you're a good writer. So my hunch was that you revealed a bit of how you felt about your marriage, that it wasn't flowery romance but more of a business proposition, that it was something you felt you were expected to do. It was part of the whole 'good son' package."

"But my father didn't approve of Julia, since she and her family were slaveholders."

"So, it was a tweak at your father," said Sam. "You could have chosen any girl you wanted. You were handsome enough, and a good rider, and hardworking. But you chose this particular girl, so perhaps it was a statement of sorts to your father."

"I hadn't looked at it that way," said Grant. He smiled wryly. "But you are right about the lack of romance. I got better at playing the part of the devoted husband after many years, but I know my track record was pretty bad there for the first seventeen years of marriage."

"And you never got to do what you wanted to do with your life," commented Sam. "You know, it brings to mind the other major influence in your life."

"Who?" asked Grant, mentally drawing a blank.

"Your father, Jesse. Maybe, since you weren't the son he wanted you to be in terms of this patriotic hero, in your heart, you figured you didn't deserve to succeed at anything else, anything that wasn't what he had wanted for you. So all those business ideas failed, and you ended up in the War of the Rebellion."

"Where I succeeded brilliantly," said Grant. "Even my worst critics said so."

"True, from a military point of view, but at a huge cost to your soul. Remember, you've spent over a hundred years being tormented by the ghosts of that period of your life, since most, if not all, of the ghosts are from your military days," said Sam.

"So since being what they wanted me to be wasn't what I wanted, my brain made me fail at everything that wasn't what Julia or my father would have approved of. Hmmm," considered Grant. "That's really sad."

"So, coveting doesn't really work for us," said Sam. "It's better to figure out what you want to do with your life, what you want to be, and give yourself permission to do it and to be happy doing it. God's commandments are a great set of guidelines to help us find our happiness. Adultery will not lead to marital happiness, and it is in our close relationship with another person, like marriage, that we learn so much about ourselves."

"God must feel really strongly about the adultery thing," said Grant, "Since he mentions it twice, once in the commandment about not committing adultery, and again in this commandment about not coveting."

"He does feel strongly about it," said Sam. "People need to choose as wisely as they can the partner with whom they will spend their life. Ideally, they should choose a good friend who will accompany them on their journey through life, as they grow, with each of them continuing to grow, and growing together, through shared experiences, such as the lessons they have learned together, the children they have raised, the dreams they have shared, and the places they have been."

"What about couples that fight all the time?" asked Grant.

"That's probably what they are used to, what their parents' marriages were like," replied Sam. "They must want it to be like that, or they'd change and decide to live in harmony. Something attracted them to each other in the beginning, and something usually keeps such couples together. Sometimes the anger is the issue they need to work on, in the safety of a long-term relationship. But they need to be careful to not let the anger get out of control, to not hurt each other or their children, to remember that each of us has some of God in us, and to not lose sight of that."

"That's a really good way of looking at marriage and its struggles," said Grant.

"Thank you," said Sam, smiling. He continued, "The tenth commandment is God's way of saying that people need to accept what they have; that they need to appreciate that they already have everything they need in order to learn. We don't actually <u>need</u> a big fancy house or a fast sports car or fancy clothing. We may want them, but we don't need them. Our survival is not imperiled if we don't have a house that our friends admire. The real person is <u>within</u> each of us, not in the outer trappings. Coveting leads us down a false path regarding what is important."

"Poor Julia," said Grant. "I feel sorry for her. Most of her life was coveting. She wanted a hero for a husband, a big elegant house that would be the envy of her friends, beautiful elegant clothing, the finest furnishings for the house, everything that was the best and finest. It's a shame we couldn't have just lived in our hand-built cabin on our hundred acres and been poor and happy. I'd still have had the ghosts from the Mexican War, but nothing like what I've endured since then."

"I know," soothed Sam. "But Julia's spirit has to work through those issues on her own, to discover that money isn't everything, that people can be happy with the barest of essentials. God always provides for our needs. It's when our wants get in the way and become a ruling force in our lives that there are problems."

Grant linked this to another commandment. "So

money becomes a false god, too. This whole elegant lifestyle thing can become a false god."

"Absolutely," said Sam. "Some people's houses are a veritable shrine to the false god of home furnishings. I've seen people whose closets are like that too, packed with more clothing than they'll ever wear in a lifetime, lots of it with the tags still on it. Always sort out what you need in order to survive, compared to what you want, and what is excessive. You need a roof over your head, but not a mansion that swamps a person with mortgage payments so that they constantly worry over money and skimp on food for themselves and their children."

Grant looked back at Timothy Rawlins and his magnificent steed one last time. "But I still like good horses," he said.

Sam chuckled.

Chapter 14

The Body is the Temple of the Lord

"So," said Sam as he began their lesson one day, "Have you ever heard the phrase 'The Body is the Temple of the Lord'?"

Grant nodded.

"What do you think it means?" asked Sam.

"That God gives us our body and we should take good care of it, like keeping clean, for Cleanliness is Next to Godliness, as my mother used to say," said Grant.

"Okay, that's a start. God gives us our human bodies for when we're on earth, and yes, it's a good idea to take care of them to the best of our ability. Our body is also the carrier, if you will, of our spirit, which lives eternal. That's how we're talking right now, because after you died, your spirit left the body that had housed it for so long, and came to this plane, where you are now."

Grant nodded.

"Let's consider first what are healthy things to put into our bodies," said Sam.

"That's pretty easy," replied Grant. "Healthy foods, like meat and potatoes and vegetables. Oh, and coffee and tobacco were two of my other favorites."

"Coffee is probably okay in moderation," said Sam, "But what about tobacco? Was there anything in your life that might suggest that tobacco wasn't too good for your body?"

"You mean like the cancer of the throat that tortured me and then killed me?" said Grant. "You think that was due to the tobacco? I always thought it was due to that peach I was eating one day during the summer of 1884. I thought the fruit had hurt my throat."

"I definitely think it was due to the tobacco," replied Sam. "You had smoked for many many years, and that's one of the risks of smoking. I think the cancer was already there and growing when the peach lodged against it, causing pain. Besides, I've never heard of a peach causing throat cancer. Nonetheless, you didn't go to a doctor about it until October that year. The doctor found your soft palate was inflamed, dark and scaly, suggestive of an epithelial problem. There was also a hard patch on the base of the right side of your tongue. The doctor treated it by lessening congestion and odors from the ulcerated area, and reduced the pain with topical cocaine. You gave up cigars, and had a tooth extracted as well."

"You really seem to know a lot about my medical history," commended Grant.

Sam smiled. "I've always been good at research, and in order to help someone, you need as much information as possible," he said.

"By February 1885, the ulcer was more active," continued Sam, "And the doctor finally got a biopsy, which showed epithelioma or epithelial cancer, as you know."

"And I rejected the idea of surgery," said Grant. "They wanted to cut out a big chunk of me, and I wanted to write my memoirs so that I could provide for Julia. Do you think if they'd biopsied it back when it first hurt in the summer of 1884, that I might have lived longer?"

"Maybe," said Sam, "But no one knows for sure. There weren't many treatments for cancer back then, like there are now. Even now, survival rates are very variable. I think it has to do with whether one is ready to move on from the current lifetime, as to how much energy a person gives to the treatment of cancer. These days, I see a lot of people who had chemotherapy and/or radiation and their hair falls out and they spend much of the last months or years of their life feeling wretchedly ill, just to live an extra year. But, in summary, tobacco wasn't a good idea. What about your other weakness?"

"You mean chocolate?" joked Grant.

The ghost of John Rawlins floated by. "Alcohol," he whispered to Grant, as helpful in death as he had been in life.

Grant sighed. Alcohol. It had played such a significant role in his life, a friend who could help him forget the reality of his life, the intense sorrow at always doing what others expected him to do and to be, and at never really being free to just be himself, a humble professor of mathematics.

He had even promised Julia's father he would

become a professor back when he had been courting the planter's daughter. Colonel Dent had said that his daughter Julia was not cut out for the life of a soldier's wife, that she was not the sort to be happy in that life, and so Grant had promised that he would accept the college professorship that he had been offered in Hillsboro, Ohio. But then the Mexican War had come along, and the academic opening "evaporated." Grant had remained in the army, and eventually had gotten leave and come home and married Julia.

"I hate to interrupt your reverie," said Sam.

Grant shook his head, as if to clear away the memories.

"How old were you when you first started drinking?" asked Sam.

"Well," considered Grant, "Are we counting things like cider and the hot toddies my mother would give me when I was ill, and the eggnog at Christmas?"

Sam nodded. "Yes, those are all forms of alcohol."

"Then, I guess I was pretty young, grammar school maybe."

"And how did it make you feel back then?" asked

Sam.

"It burned my throat. I hated the taste," replied Grant.

"So at what point did your feelings about alcohol and its effects change?" Sam asked gently.

"On the way to West Point, I think. I was afraid of disgracing my father by failing at West Point, the way Dr. Bailey's son had. The only good thing I could see about going there was that I would get to visit the two great cities of the continent, Philadelphia and New York. After I visited them en route to college, I would have been glad to have had a steamboat or railroad collision, or any other accident, by which I might have been injured and therefore not eligible to attend the Academy. But nothing of the sort happened, and I had to face the music."

"So you found alcohol?" asked Sam.

"Yes, on the canal ride from Pittsburgh to Harrisburg, one of the other travelers and I got to talking. He was a young fellow like me, and had spent most of his life at boarding school. His name was Joe, if I recall, and his mother had died when he was very young. When his father remarried, the new wife didn't want Joe around to remind his father of his father's first wife, and Joe had been packed off to boarding school. That's where he learned to drink. Then he gave me a taste of this whiskey he had in a silver flask. It burned like anything going down, since it was raw spirits, but a few minutes later I felt better than I had in a long time. I was feeling no pain. That sorrow about my life was gone, along with my dread of reaching my destination. I was able to forget that a military life had no charms for me and that I had not the faintest idea of staying in the army, even if I should be graduated. I even forgot about my father, and his anger. It was incredible. It was like finding out that I could be free, except when it wore off." Grant sighed in his customary way.

"What happened when it wore off?" enquired Sam.

"I'd be more depressed than ever," said Grant. "Nonetheless, alcohol was a good friend at school, especially since most of my roommates also drank. Had to keep it well hidden so we didn't get any demerits, of course."

"And you kept drinking?"

"Yes, it was part of the social scene as young officers, after we graduated and ranked where we would like to be stationed and in what unit after we graduated. There's always a lot of drinking by the officers. It helps pass the time, and relieve the boredom," said Grant.

"And before you knew it, you were hooked," commented Sam, in a nonjudgmental and matter-of-fact tone.

"I suppose," said Grant. "I figured I could quit whenever I wanted to, and several times I stopped drinking for a week or two, just to see if I could. And since I could stop, and didn't have any withdrawal, I figured it was safe."

"But it wasn't," said Sam. "When did you find you couldn't stop?"

"After I came back from Mexico and got married. We moved often, and alcohol was the one constant thing in my life. Julia never said anything against it, so I figured it was okay with her if I drank."

"Do you think there might be some connection between getting married and your increasing use of alcohol?" asked Sam.

"No, I loved Julia. I wrote to her all the time during the Mexican War. She waited for me for four long years. I couldn't back out and refuse to marry her. She was pretty old by that point, waiting for me," said Grant.

"But she was the daughter of a wealthy planter," said Sam. "She had always had lots of suitors, and she would have found someone else if you hadn't wanted to marry her."

"To tell you the truth, and I've never ever told anyone else this, I didn't want to get married. Not to Julia, not to anyone. But I had to get married, to prove I was 'normal' if you know what I mean. Everyone got married in those days, or they thought there was something wrong with you. Besides, my parents wanted grandchildren."

"That's an interesting excuse," said Sam. "You had two other brothers who could provide grandchildren for your parents, to carry on the family name and lineage. Suddenly other events in your life begin to make more sense. I feel really bad for you, Grant, endlessly trapped in situations not of your choosing. It's really sad."

"You're telling me," said Grant. "So I drank to forget. And when I drank, sometimes I got into mischief. Like that whole fiasco with Helen, the blond-haired wife of that one lieutenant. I wasn't really attracted to her, but I did have needs and that looked like a socially acceptable choice. Besides, she practically threw herself at me. It would have insulted her to refuse."

Sam shook his head. "And to further complicate your life, then you got involved in bad money deals where you were swindled out of your money out there."

"Yes, the first was a friend of Helen's, who had been with us on the trip through Panama, before Helen died, and then the second time was with her husband. I didn't want him to suspect that I had ever been involved with his wife, so I had to trust him."

"No," said Sam, "You had to trust in God and the codes for behavior that God assigned, the Commandments we've been working on. As we've seen, adultery is so wrong that God has not one but two commandments about it. Maybe you lost the money as a way of punishing yourself."

"I hadn't thought about it, but that sounds right. And then I drank to forget about it, since I knew that Julia would be hurt, and her father would be angry at me, as would my father. My father never once cheated on my mother. I was nothing but a big louse," said Grant, as big invisible tears welled up in his eyes.

Sam sat silently and allowed Grant to feel these emotions and to process his behavior. After a very long time, Sam finally spoke, to say, "It is good to realize the effects of your behavior on others. No man is an island. We are all part of a larger whole, be it a family, a community, a town, a state, a country or a planet. We affect them, and they affect us. You cannot heal a wound in your spirit until you have found the wound and know that it _is_ a wound. From our greatest pain comes our greatest growth."

Grant felt himself becoming calmer, and that familiar faint infusion of hope came to him. "Then I won't always feel this bad about the things I did?"

Sam reassured him, as he had done many times before. "No. As you grow, you will see these things as growing pains, to use a phrase. It doesn't make what you did right, but you can use these experiences as stepping stones to getting healthier spiritually, to finding the path home to God and walking as close as possible to that path."

"I did so much when I was drinking," said Grant. "And I knew I shouldn't drink. I really fooled some of them though. Like that Reverend Crane. He used to tell everyone how I was always cheerful, that no toil, cold, heat, hunger, fatigue or lack of money ever depressed me.

He never knew that I was the very personification of the word depressed. There were many times I thought myself to be the sorriest lot on earth, the very saddest sack who somehow managed to get himself up out of bed and stumble through another painful day."

Sam listened quietly as Grant reminisced.

"He never knew how afraid I was, like the conflict with Harris at Florida, Missouri, at the start of the Rebellion," continued Grant. "My heart was in my mouth, I was terrified, but I didn't have the moral courage to halt and consider what to do, so I just kept going. Of course, I found out that Harris had been just as afraid of me as I was of him, but I was afraid. A great soldier and leader should never be afraid. When I felt scared, the alcohol was there for me."

"And then, there was the time on one of our marches that some of the boys broke away from the lines and filled their canteens with whiskey. Soon they were reeling along under the influence. So I told the regiment that we were stopping to rest, and then I went through the ranks and took each canteen and sniffed it. I dumped all those containing alcohol onto the ground, and had the offenders tied behind the baggage wagons until they sobered into soldierly propriety. I never allowed any whiskey or intoxicating beverages in camp. That minister thought I was the biggest teetotaler around." Grant shook his head. "The irony of it."

"Sometimes, we're hardest on those who have faults that remind us of our own faults," said Sam. "For instance, the most militant anti-smoking people are usually those who used to be smokers themselves. The child we usually argue most with in our home is often the one who is most like ourselves. So it doesn't surprise me that you would get that angry about alcohol. You yourself took pains never to drink in camp."

"I guess that was kind of hypocritical, wasn't it," asked Grant. "To set a no-alcohol rule, and then go out of camp to break it. Maybe I should have just allowed it in camp, but then the soldiers would have been undisciplined."

"Maybe abstaining would have been the best solution," suggested Sam.

"The irony is that I kept drinking, whenever I could or when I really needed it. I thought I could control it, even though alcohol was what got me discharged from the Army in 1854. I resigned to avoid being court-martialed for being intoxicated while on duty," said Grant.

Sam continued to listen.

"Others noticed my drinking, too. Like that Captain Kountz," said Grant.

"The one you said was a big troublemaker, interfering with the telegrams between you and General Halleck," said Sam.

Grant nodded. "Kountz came to see me one day in camp, to discuss his plans, and I wanted him to just take care of the matter himself and to stop interrupting me since I was working on some other large issues at the time. He wouldn't take the hint. He just kept going on and on, not listening to what I was saying. My head ached. It was awful. I just wanted him to go and to leave me alone."

"Maybe he didn't want to take responsibility for the course of action he was considering," suggested Sam.

Grant considered this thoughtfully, stroking the beard that no longer appeared in fleshly form. "Probably right," he said. "So then, General Rawlins put him out of my office. Kountz then went around proclaiming that General Grant and his staff were all drunk. It was terrible. Rawlins would never ever drink. His father had been an alcoholic, like my grandfather had. Rawlins had the strongest abhorrence of the stuff of anyone I ever met."

"The best way to avoid getting hooked on something when there's a family weakness for it is to never start using it," commented Sam.

"True," said Grant. "What my mother used to say about an ounce of prevention is worth a pound of cure." He fell silent, into a reverie for a few moments, and then resumed the thread of his story. "So, my good friend Colonel Hillyer then placed Captain Kountz under arrest. I felt bad about the whole thing, since Kountz was just trying to do his job, and I ordered that Kountz be released. Not one of my better ideas," said Grant. "Kountz was malignant ever after in his behavior, interrupting the telegrams, and bad-mouthing me to anyone who would listen."

"So, were you drunk at the time?" asked Sam, cutting to the key part of the matter.

"Of course," chuckled Grant. "There's no smoke without fire somewhere."

"Ulysses, Ulysses," said Sam, shaking his head. "At least you're honest about it."

"Then there's the whole fiasco at Shiloh," said Grant, reminiscing again. "Not only was I drunk, and it almost ended my army career, but I ended up at a dance hall with a woman, undressed, and it almost ended my marriage. That would have been a total 'crash and burn' to use a phrase I learned from a pilot I met here. You know, I look back at my life and I can't believe I did that. There are times I was just so self-destructive it's a miracle I survived, let alone led the Union to victory."

Sam nodded. "A lot of times we are our own worst enemy. We always need to be on the watch against things that can distract us from our true purpose. Things like alcohol, and drugs, and other addictions, like gambling, that take our energy away from our families and our work. Even work can be an addiction, if it causes you to neglect your family, and takes up too much of your energy."

"Guilty of that one, for sure," said Ulysses. "Julia and I were apart more often than together for most of the first seventeen years of our marriage. That's why I think she enjoyed our tour of Europe so much, that we were together. But I was never comfortable with all that togetherness stuff. Maybe I should have given farming a second chance. Maybe I'd have been better off alone for a good part of the day."

"And yet you had wanted to be a professor of mathematics, and a teacher, by definition, has students," said Sam. "Maybe it's not being around people that was the problem, but the responsibilities and the expectations that those people had for you."

Grant considered this. "You're right. The people around me have always wanted something. My father wanted me to be a soldier, a credit to his patriotic fantasies, a West Point graduate. My mother just expected me to be quiet, well-behaved, and to not get into any trouble. Julia expected me to be famous. The people in the army expected me to win. When I was president, people were always expecting favors."

"Even Julia was always expecting favors," continued Grant. "Every time she'd visit, she'd have some hard luck story or another about one of her secesher friends, like the one whose father had been verbally abusive to Union troops and who'd been asked to leave. His daughter came crying to Julia that it would 'jes kill poor ole Pappa if he were put out of his home'," said Grant, imitating a Southern drawl. "So, I had to caution the old man, and allow him to stay in his home, provided he made no further trouble. Then there was some secesh widow whose husband died at Vicksburg, and the widow wanted to go visit her husband's friends in Georgia, all of them rebels, and she didn't have any money. Julia had known her from years ago, and had recently received over $4,000 in Confederate money as a souvenir from one of our campaigns. So Julia gave this woman the whole packet of money. Of course, guilt overcame my poor Julia and she came to me later and told me the whole tale of what she had done, but what could I do but forgive her?"

"Always something," said Sam.

"And every time Julia visited, she would see the sick and wounded, and beg me to allow them to go home. I dealt with that all week, when she wasn't here; it wasn't fair that I should have to deal with it when she was visiting as well. Even one of her Rebel brothers, who had been taken prisoner, she tried to get me to trade prisoners so he could come home, and I had to tell her that that I could not do. Personally, I thought it served him right. Demands, demands, demands."

"And yet you loved her," said Sam, with a faint question to his voice.

"I suppose so," said Grant. "As much as I loved anyone, I guess. I can't say that I really know what love is, or what it feels like. My own childhood wasn't full of that warm fuzzy lovey-dovey stuff that I've seen some parents do with their children. All gitchy-gooey and 'You're so sweet' and hugs and kisses. My family wasn't like that, and neither was Julia's. But she was always there for me, and I guess she was faithful, although there always were male admirers hanging around her, like Admiral Farragut, and her cousin, Pete Longstreet. But Pete was her cousin, and I'm sure she wouldn't have been involved with him. I wouldn't have blamed her if she had been unfaithful. I mean, I was no paragon of virtue either, and I was hardly ever home. So who knows?" said Grant.

Sam nodded. "Who knows, indeed. So let's wrap up for today. We've covered the fact that the Body is the Temple of the Lord, and we should take care of it, and feed it healthy foods, and not put unhealthy substances into it, like alcohol and tobacco. We should watch out for other addictions as well."

Grant nodded. "Wait," he said. "Before you go today, there's something else I want to ask on this subject. Do you think I had cancer of the throat, the throat being an integral part of how a person speaks, at least the way I understand it, because there were so many things in my life I either didn't say or couldn't say?"

Sam nodded thoughtfully and considered this. "That's certainly a possibility. I've seen lots of women, for instance, develop breast cancer when they are extremely upset about something pertaining to their family, and the breast of course is the symbol of nurturing. So, I do think it's a possibility. What do you wish you would have said other than what you put in your memoirs?"

"Well, I should have spoken up to my parents and chosen the path in my life that I wanted. I would have spared myself all those years of anguish and misery. And I think I should have been honest with myself during my courtship of Julia, and not gotten married. I should have been honest with myself about my drinking, and gotten help when I needed it. Then my thinking would have been clearer, and maybe Shiloh and the Wilderness and Cold Harbor would never have happened. All those people wouldn't have died. Actually, if I'd gone my own way back before going to West Point, I wouldn't have been involved in any of it. That would have been a tremendous relief."

Grant drifted off into his thoughts, and Sam sat silently, waiting to see what his student said next.

"You know," said Grant with a sigh, "I had these great friends who always did what they could to cover for me. Like Cadwallader and Dana. They both knew I drank far too much, like that trip to Satartia where I was really on a drunk, for days, and they covered for me. They never said or wrote anything about it until after I died. Sometimes I'd go back down to earth to see what people I had known were doing or saying, and I remember how upset people were when they found out about that Satartia incident. And by then, I had no way of telling people that it was true, that it was something I myself should have owned up to. My grandson, in particular, used to get so angry about the alcohol issue; he only wanted to think about me as a military hero. He could never see or understand my immense pain at having lived a life not of my choosing, at always being and doing what other people wanted me to do. My grandson, like so many people, never understood my sorrow, my grief."

"I know," said Sam. "I can see it right away in the photographs of you. But you're right; people see what they want to see. And it's easier for people to see you as a military hero than it is for them to look at the much bigger issue that war is wrong and that hundreds of thousands of lives were lost in a war that should never have progressed to a war. It should have been sorted out peacefully long before that point."

"And what about my friends?" asked Grant. "If they had spoken up when I was alive, maybe I would have gotten the help I needed."

"Maybe, but probably not. You took the Temperance Pledge once, and fell off the wagon so to speak. So you knew you had a problem. It was up to you to fix it, and that would be a heavy burden indeed to place on your friends. They were trying to be helpful, especially Rawlins, who was very clear in his anti-alcohol message to you. I doubt he could have made it any clearer. But you chose to ignore him. Lots of times, we send messengers like Rawlins into people's lives with specific messages that they need to hear. But we can't make people listen to the messages."

"True," said Grant. "Rawlins told me over and over again. He was always honest with me. The other soldiers and officers used to make fun of Rawlins and I, saying that Rawlins was guilty of insubordination on a daily basis, but he was like my conscience. I put up with it, and even encouraged it, because part of me knew I needed to listen to what Rawlins was saying. And I think a part of me took pleasure in finding ways to get around what he was saying. And I feel bad about not praising him more in my memoirs. We had a falling out, and I don't even remember the details, it was so trivial. I am really sorry I slighted such a loyal friend that way."

"Then go to him, and make it right," suggested Sam. "Tell him how you valued his friendship and advice, and how you are sorry you didn't listen better. And tell him you feel bad that you didn't write more about him in your memoirs. I think it will go a long way to helping Rawlins to move on, since this is the big issue on which he is stuck. He tried so hard to help you, and feels he didn't succeed in a lot of ways."

"But he succeeded in ways he never knew," said Grant. "I loved him like he was my own brother."

"And it's okay to tell him that," said Sam. "Here in the realm of spirit, we can express things like that, things that may not have been able to be said back in the second half of the nineteenth century."

"But just because a man wouldn't say that sort of thing doesn't make it right that I never told him how much I valued him," said Grant. "This I can fix. I can make this right."

"Good," said Sam, smiling serenely. "Then let's stop here for today. I'll see you, hmmm, let's see, the day after tomorrow. That should give you the time you need," said Sam, as he drifted off.

Grant sat for a long time, thinking about this most recent topic, and reminiscing about the various events in his life. He tried to imagine a better life, one in which he had been free to do as he wished, where no one made any demands on him, but he doubted that such a life existed. He pictured those who had been his friends, and resolved that tomorrow he would set forth to make things right with them, starting with John Rawlins. Comforted with warm feelings about the people in his life who had been there for him, he drifted off to sleep.

In his dream, he was traveling through old corridors, with marble floors. The building was an old one, by modern standards, for Grant was aware that it was now somewhere in the 1990s. Glass cases, with all kinds of war memorabilia on display--muskets and rifles and cartridge boxes. Civil War drums. Things from other wars, like World War I and World War II. Grant knew about those from soldiers he had met up here, soldiers who had been killed and who were angry at their commanding officers for letting them be killed, through bad tactics or just bad luck. War takes lives, and each of those lives was an individual matter. He was learning that now.

Grant floated along the corridor with interest. A room labeled the Gettysburg Room. How interesting. He floated through the locked door into the large room, with its portraits of military people on the walls, local people of wherever he was, he didn't recognize any of them. He smiled as he saw the old cannon in the middle of the room, mounted on its wooden carrier. The cannon gleamed in the faint reflected light that came through the tiny windows with their iron bars. Grant floated over to the cannon and touched it lovingly.

Something caught his eye, and he turned to the left. There, in a display case, was the chair, his chair, the one he kept seeing, the one in his dreams. Well, this was a dream, too, he thought, but this time, the chair was in context. He floated over to the chair to see it better. There was a little switch on the case, and Grant turned it on, using all the force he could muster, for it was much harder to produce a physical action in spirit form. Ah, now he could see it better. His chair. The seat was well-worn, the grain of the wood rough and exposed. It had been handmade for him, and the arms curved down and the seat sloped back so that Grant could rest in his favorite pose. The chair had fitted him like a glove. If only he could sit in it again.

He looked at the chair, trying to see if there was a way to get it out, to sit on it. Someone had painted a picture of him on it, and in gold letters had written, "General Grant's Chair. Made for Headquarters at Chattanooga. Used by Him during His Stay. Owned by _______ Dufder, Esq. For 34 years." Some of the letters were faded and impossible to read. There was a piece broken off the left top of the chair, and a round hole in the left arm of the chair, where it had been struck by a stray bullet one time. Fortunately, Grant hadn't been in the chair at the time.

Grant thought a moment. He had been able to float through the locked doors; maybe he could get through the case. It would feel so good to sit in his chair again. He closed his eyes and concentrated, picturing himself sitting in the chair, the way some of the other ghosts had taught him.

There, he was in. If he were still human, he'd be gasping for air, but there were some advantages to being a ghost, thought Grant, smiling faintly to himself at his morbid humor. He stretched out in the chair, and lit a cigar, puffing contentedly for several hours.

The next morning, at Soldiers and Sailors Memorial Hall, Dr. Richard Sanders, the Curator, was on his way to his office at seven forty-five in the morning when he noticed a light on in the Gettysburg Room, which was locked.

"I better go get the keys. Someone must have left a light on accidentally yesterday, and the lock-up crew missed it," the curator thought to himself.

He took the ancient elevator to his office on the second floor. As he walked through the corridors, he admired the high ceilings and polished marble floors. It was a lovely building, he reflected, a perfect place to house the memorabilia of the Allegheny County veterans who had faithfully served their country. Dr. Sanders dropped off his briefcase and lunch tote in his office, got out the key he needed, and went down to the Gettysburg Room.

The curator opened the door, and the smell of cigar smoke assailed his nostrils. It wasn't the same smell as the cigarettes that the building manager smoked; it was almost perfumey. "They really need to outlaw smoking in the museum," thought the curator, shaking his head.

He looked around the room, trying to see if anything was amiss. He noticed that the case containing Grant's chair was lit; someone must have turned on the little light that was inside the case in order to see the chair better. Phew, thought the curator, the smoke is really strong here.

A thought came unbidden into Richard's head. Back when he had been transcribing the letters of Milton McJ., a Civil War soldier, he had smelled pipe smoke every night for months. At that time, Richard and his wife and daughter were living in a half of a twin house, with a

thick stone wall separating the two houses. Their land-
lords lived in the other half. Richard had thought for
months that old Hank had taken up smoking a pipe, just to
aggravate the Sanders, and the Sanders had eventually
found a house to buy a few blocks away, and had moved
out. The smell had followed them, and only went away
after Richard was done transcribing the letters and had
sent them back to the man who owned them, Richard's
friend Dominic.

"Hmmm," thought the curator, stroking his beard
thoughtfully. "I wonder....". He reflected on the fact that
Grant had smoked cigars, and had in fact died of cancer of
the throat.

The curator turned off the light in the case containing Grant's chair, looked around the room to be sure
nothing else was amiss, and went back to his office.

Sam arrived just as Grant was waking up. As
usual, Grant sensed the light and warmth before he
actually saw his mentor.

"I had the most amazing dream," said Grant. "I
found my old chair, the one I keep seeing and thinking
about. The one that was made for me at Chattanooga. It's

in an old museum in Pittsburgh, of all places. Actually not too far from my native Ohio."

"Hmmm," said Sam. "That's nice, that you found your old chair. Do you think it has some significance?"

"I don't know," replied Grant, stretching. "So what is today's topic?"

"Well, we're heading for the home stretch, and there are only a few more points to go over. Today we're going to talk about Jesus' message, and the two main teachings that He taught."

"Jesus' message--that's easy. It's all in the New Testament," said Grant. "But that's too obvious. I bet I'm missing something here."

Sam chuckled. "You're really getting good at this. Yes, the New Testament is a collection of some of the things that Jesus said, to the best recollection of the writers, who began writing it down long after Jesus was killed."

"How long?"

"Thirty years or more," replied Sam, "To the best of my knowledge."

Grant sighed. "I know how hard it was to write my memoirs twenty years after the War of the Rebellion.

I had my son Fred go over every single fact to be sure I got them all right. And I had the Official Records to help me, and the writing that Adam Badeau had done, and the notes that John Rawlins had kept. I had all these things to help me and it was still a challenge."

"That's a good analogy," affirmed Sam. "Matthew, Mark and John were all apostles; they had lived and worked with Jesus and had been there when he spoke. Luke was a Greek physician, and he arrived about a week after Jesus had been killed. He never actually got to meet the man he had heard so much about. Luke interviewed Jesus' mother and the apostles and Mary Magdalene and others in order to write his gospel. And there are other gospels that were written that have been suppressed because they don't agree with the dogma that certain churches are teaching. So they have hidden away these older documents in favor of new fabrications. Like the whole thing about not eating meat on Fridays. That's an invention of the church. Besides, they eat fish, and fish is an animal and therefore a meat. Millions of fish lose their lives because of this little bit of invention by humans. But, I don't want to get too far off the track. Much of the rest of the New Testament was written by Saul, who changed his name to Paul when he was confronted by God and decided to stop persecuting the followers of Christ. There is actually some historic documentation that Jesus was stoned and that Paul participated in that. But I wasn't there at the time."

Grant nodded, listening intently.

"So, then, what are the two main teachings of Jesus?" Sam asked.

"You want me to boil it all down to two teachings? There were dozens of parables and stories and lessons. How do I pick out the most important?"

"We look for themes, and we need to consider the fact that Jesus was a Jewish rabbi and think about some of what the Jewish religion teaches," said Sam.

"I must confess I know very little if anything about the Jewish religion," said Grant. "Other than what you've taught me."

"Well, for starters, a fundamental Jewish prayer is something called the Sh'ma. And it says, Hear O Israel, The Lord our God, The Lord is One. And that is a fundamental truth, throughout all the religions of the world. The God to whom each religion prays is the same God. He or She is interpreted a bit differently, and there are different rituals, but the basic stories are the same. There is One True Creator who created everything."

"Makes a lot of sense," said Grant. He stroked his beard thoughtfully. "So it really didn't matter if I went to the Lutheran church or the Methodist or the Episcopalian?"

"No, it didn't matter," said Sam. "The same God is prayed to in all houses of worship. You could even have gone to a synagogue or a mosque or a Hindu temple. There is One God, and that is one of the teachings of Jesus."

"So Union and Confederate soldiers were all created by the same God," said Grant.

"As people yes; they weren't born as soldiers," agreed Sam. "And the Christians and the Saracens in the Crusades were all children of the same God. And the Persians and the Greeks, the lesson I myself had to learn, at great price."

"Does it apply across the globe, then?" asked Grant.

Sam nodded. "Yes, no matter what people's nationality or religion or race or creed or sex or color or any other characteristic, we are all children of the same

God. And so are all the other beings that God created, like insects and birds and horses and flowers."

"And Jesus' second teaching?" asked Grant.

"That we should Love One Another as he loved us. He said this a number of times, including at the last supper, which as you may know was actually his celebration of the Jewish festival of Passover, which commemorates the exodus of the Jewish slaves from Egypt, led by Moses. Ironically though, Moses survived to lead the people through the desert and to the promised land, and Jesus was crucified because of man's inhumanity to man. No one stepped forward to help Jesus or to save him."

"But it's written in the Bible that that was how he would die."

"A horrible, painful death that they used on criminals was used on this gifted prophet and teacher that God sent to earth to carry God's divine message. One of God's children, treated so cruelly by others, and not one person stepped forward to help him. No matter what was written, someone could have, or should have, stepped forward to help this man. There weren't all that many Roman soldiers there; Jesus' followers could have banded together and overthrown the soldiers, without much difficulty at all. But they chose to see an innocent man be killed, rather than to speak up. So now, every year at Christmas and Easter, people sing songs in all the churches about how sad it is that no one knew back then how significant Jesus was, that He was the Son of God, etcetera, etcetera. And in modern time, if these so-called good Christians were to meet a prophet like Jesus, they wouldn't recognize him. They'd be more likely to scoff at him or her, to insult him, and to make his job more difficult at work, that sort of thing."

"Jesus washed the feet of his disciples at the last supper they shared," continued Sam, "and told them that they should love one another as He loved them--in other words, unconditionally. He showed them how his body would be broken and his blood spilled because of man's lack of understanding and love. People need to understand that they are not 'saved' as a result of Jesus' death, but that they must make sure they are not modern counterparts of those that contributed to His death. When we say that Jesus 'died for our sins,' it means he died because of the collective sins of all those people who contributed to his death, both those who actively killed him and those who passively sat back and allowed it to occur. He didn't have to die. And it wasn't just the High Priests and Roman government people that contributed to Jesus' death. Every one of those townspeople who said 'Kill him' is guilty. Every one of Jesus' followers who didn't speak out is guilty. Every human being who allowed such a massive injustice to be perpetrated against one of God's creations is guilty. And they must all answer for their actions. Jesus' death was the ultimate symbol of man's cruelty and inhumanity to man. No one stepped forward to save him. We need to work towards a better world in which such a thing would not happen again."

Grant stroked his beard thoughtfully. "Well, for my part, I will never again enter the military. And I will do my best to work for a better world, a world based on kindness."

"Now," said Sam, "You need to think about examples in which you showed love for another human being, a sense of selflessness, of wanting to help just to do something nice, not for personal gain."

Grant thought about this for a long moment. "Well, when Captain Howard was killed one week after Galena's first company was raised, I paid for the college education of his two sons. I sent one to Annapolis and one to West Point."

"Which would seem to be a generous gesture," said Sam. "Of course, the two boys were devastated at the thought of the military, since that was how their father had died."

Grant felt as if he were a balloon that had just come in contact with a tack. An immense wave of sadness flooded over him and his eyes grew misty with unshed tears. "I had no idea," he said in a whisper. "I just wanted to see that they would get an education, as their father would have done for them if he had lived."

"And that part of your gesture was good," said Sam. "But a regular college would have been a better choice, even if it had been more expensive."

Grant sighed, and the two spirits were silent for a while.

"Well," said Grant. "I can think of another example. One time, Julia asked me to pardon a man who was to be shot for going AWOL. Julia pointed out that the man had gone to see his seven-month-old baby whom he had never seen, and that the man's wife had begged him to come to see the baby. Julia argued that he shouldn't be shot for this, but should be pardoned, and against my better judgement, I pardoned him."

"Against your better judgement?" echoed Sam.

"Yes, I didn't want the other soldiers to get the wrong idea," said Grant, reverting to his old military style.

"Ulysses, Ulysses," said Sam. "When will you learn? <u>Of course</u> it was okay for the man to go see his son. It would have been better for the man to be <u>at home</u> with his wife and child anyhow. For that matter, I must remind you that it would have been better for <u>you</u> to be at home with your wife and children." Sam's voice had grown quite heated. This was a topic he felt he had gone over many times, and he was dismayed that Grant still didn't seem to get it.

"So, I guess we can't count that example," said Grant with a faint rueful twist of his lips.

"Nope," said Sam.

Grant thought and thought. "I need to lend this more thought. Can I have another hour?"

"Of course," said Sam. "I'll be back then." And the light faded as Sam took his leave.

Grant sat there, thinking. A vision of Pete Long-street came to him then. Wide forehead, high cheekbones, long flowing beard and those intelligent dark eyes of his. Pete, his wife's cousin, a Lieutenant General on the Confederate side back in the War of the Rebellion. But Pete had been family, sighed Grant, and so I gave him a job after the war.

Grant pondered the reasons why Pete Longstreet would pop into his head at this time. Sure, giving him a job was nice, and Sam would say that that had been very nice of Grant, but there was something more. Or was there? Grant continued to think.

An hour later, Sam arrived, true to his word. The characteristic light and warmth which accompanied him warmed Ulysses, who sat feeling anxious about a letter and a chair.

"I think I've figured it out," said Grant.

"Figured what out?" asked Sam.

"I did something to show love for another, something big. Something that concerns that chair at that museum in Pittsburgh and a letter. Come with me, and I'll show it to you. I think the answer is there."

Sam readily agreed to accompany Grant. He thought to himself that this was very unusual behavior for

Ulysses, who generally preferred to stay close to the area in which he had died, Mount McGregor, New York.

The spirits closed their eyes and focused on where they wished to go. Soon they found themselves in an old museum in Pittsburgh, with marble floors and dimly lit display cases full of military artifacts. It was just after four in the afternoon, and the light was beginning to fade. The patrons of the museum were gone for the day, Sam noted as the two spirits traveled through the corridors.

Grant stopped at a room labeled the Gettysburg Room. The door was locked, since the museum was closed for the evening. No problem there, thought Grant. Being a spirit did confer a few advantages, he thought with a wry smile.

Grant led the way to the chair. As they arrived in front of the glass display case in which it was housed, Sam spoke. "Your old chair from Chattanooga. That's very nice. It seems to be in pretty good condition, too."

"Right," said Grant. "But there is something more. I keep thinking about the chair, and about Pete Longstreet, and I'm sure there's some connection. There was a letter I wrote one time, and I didn't want Rawlins to see what I was writing, so I hid the letter under the chair, and wrote another letter to send instead, knowing that Rawlins would read it, which he did."

Sam listened quietly, glowing with the light and warmth as he always did, which was a big help in the room's waning light.

"So, I've got to see if the letter is still there. It will prove I'm not the monster people think I was, that the whole fiasco at Cold Harbor was a mistake. I meant well. I know I didn't mean for all those people to die." Grant slipped into the display case and began searching under the chair, where the two pieces of wood that formed the two sets of legs came together to support the seat of the chair.

Grant caressed the worn wood of his chair, feeling again the bullet hole. After some searching, he pulled forth a letter, and emerged from the case holding it proudly.

Grant opened the small plain paper envelope. There was no address on it. Inside were two thin sheets of writing paper. The first was a letter in a flowery feminine script.

Sam looked at the letter. "It's a letter to Julia from her friend Mary."

"Yes," said Grant. "Mary Lee was a friend of Julia's from her schooldays, in addition to being a first cousin of Robert E. Lee. Her father was Major Richard Bland Lee, Jr. This is the letter that caused me to write the other letter in the envelope. Here, I'll read it to you."

Grant smoothed out the first letter and read to Sam,

"My dearest Julia,

I hope that this letter finds you in good health. This war saddens me so greatly, to see the very destruction of the way of life we hold so dear. I do so remember the light hearted times we had as schoolgirls, and then at my coming-out party. Oh, how I yearn for those happier times. Anyway, I am writing to you on behalf of my cousin on my father's side, Robert, who is presently engaged as a general fighting on behalf of the Confederate states against your Ulysses in this most dreadful war. I do wish there were something we ladies could do, if not to stop this whole war, then to at least see that our loved ones are returned safely home. What I wish to ask, then, is this- -do you think it possible that you might ask Ulysses to keep from harming so many people? I will do my part on this side, and write to cousin Robert. Also, your cousin

James (Pete) is working with Robert, and I have heard through some very close friends who can be trusted that he is planning to write to Ulysses about this idea. I understand that your General Ord, who works with Ulysses, is also in favor of this idea.

I pray to God for the health and safety of all our loved ones.

Your friend,

Mary"

Grant sat silently after reading the letter to his mentor.

Finally, Sam spoke. "Wow. And no one has ever seen this letter, or knows what went on behind the scenes."

Placing the second letter on top of the first, and smoothing it out, Grant said, "I know. And this one, the reply I drafted, is even more telling. I was really in a quandary about this whole thing. When Julia and I got married, my three groomsmen were Lt. Cadmus Marcellus Wilcox, Bernard Pratte of St. Louis, and Pete Longstreet. It's pretty ironic how they all ended up Confederate, and me fighting against them. Not only that, but Pete was my cousin by marriage."

Grant began to read aloud, "My dear cousin Pete,

In reply to your letter of May 15, 1864, and the beseechings on your behalf by my wife Julia and her friend, the former Mary Lee, I will do all that is in my power to see that you are returned safely to your family after the war, and that there will be as few deaths as possible. Personally, I cannot hope to imagine your reasons for wishing to fight on behalf of the confederacy, but you are family, a dear friend and a fellow schoolmate. Therefore, I wish you well, and you need have no fear on my account. Sincerely, U.S. Grant."

"Did you send the letter?" asked Sam.

Grant shook his head. "I thought about it for many days, but it seemed like a traitorous thing to do. I had a job to do for my country, and family or no family, it wouldn't have been right to send such a letter. And when Ord suggested a meeting between Julia and Pete's wife, I put my foot down and said no. Ironic, since it probably would have worked better than any battle, to let the ladies iron out the differences over tea."

"What intrigues me is that although you never sent the letter, you didn't destroy it either," said Sam. "You were a smoker. You could have crumbled it up and burnt the letter in an ashtray. But instead, you kept it somewhere safe, somewhere where it wouldn't be detected. Maybe you wanted people to know about it and this was your way of telling them."

Grant nodded. "How could I ever admit to such a thing, though? I was a national hero, a fierce warrior."

"But it's touching that you would allow a place in your heart to consider the safety of your friend and cousin, even if his views didn't agree with yours," said his mentor.

"I should have sent it," said Grant.

"Maybe, maybe not," replied Sam. "Having the wives meet for a diplomatic tea was a better idea, but men would have felt that they were being usurped by women, that women could solve this easier and less destructively than men could. You were also a creature of your time period, and that wouldn't have sat well with the social structure of the period."

"But Julia wanted to go. She begged me," said Grant.

"And we grow too soon old and too late smart," said Sam. "Yes, had she gone and the two sides reached peace, Cold Harbor would probably not have happened. But there were many deaths up til that point, and the lessons that you personally needed to learn would have been the same irregardless. But yes, many more lives would have been spared."

"I was so foolish," said Grant. He was overcome with emotion as waves of sadness flowed over him.

Sam comforted his student, enveloping him in warmth.

"You were human, and humans make mistakes. The important thing is that you know that what you did was wrong, and you are sorry, and you will make amends, and you will never do such a thing again. And we all need to work together to create a better world, in which such things will never happen again. Never to have war or combat or people killing other people."

Grant slowly pulled himself together. He could do this, work for a better world. Nothing could erase all the wrongs he had done, he knew that, but he could work for a better future. He felt his spirit grow warmer and lighter as he thought about doing good for others, and working on God's team to help create a kinder and better world.

Chapter 16

Overview

Sam gazed for the last time at Grant's blue eyes, those incredibly sad yet kind eyes of a man who had done his best for his country but at such great personal cost to his spirit that it had just about destroyed him. A man who was human, who had made his share of mistakes, and then some, but who had been willing to reach out for help from the depths of his despair, and to listen thoughtfully to everything that his teacher had said.

"Well," said Sam, "It's time for me to be moving on, and you will be too. You will meet with the council soon, where you will get to decide which lessons you want to explore in greater depth. You can choose anything you want, any parents, any place, any period of time. Choose what <u>you</u> want to learn, where you want to go."

Grant felt an intense sense of loss, and Sam wasn't even gone yet. "I don't know what to say," he said simply.

"I know," said Sam. "Of all the spirits I've helped, I've felt closest to you. Maybe because you remind me so much of myself."

"Thank you," said Grant. "That is a phenomenal compliment from one so great as yourself."

"You're welcome," said Sam. "May I also add that you are doing much better at graciously accepting compliments?"

Grant nodded. "Do you have any last minute words of advice for me? I mean, other than what you've just said."

Sam also nodded. "Well, there are the ten commandments that we went over, the Golden Rule, and the fact that the body is the temple of the Lord. Then there are the two teachings of Jesus Christ, to Love One Another as I Have Loved You, and that There is One God, which is also one of the commandments. Finally, we need to remember to walk as close to the path of God as possible."

"Anything else?" asked Grant.

"Just remember to be open to all possibilities for growth, that there's a bit of God in every being that you meet, whether it's a person or a plant or an animal or a rock. Try not to judge. And help someone else as I have helped you," said Sam, with a twinkle in his eyes. "Good luck, and know that I will always be with you, right here, in spirit."

Grant felt a glow of warmth in his heart. He was about to express his profound gratitude to this angel, who had done so much to help him, when he noticed that Sam's spirit was beginning to glow as bright as the brightest sun imaginable.

"I know," Grant felt Sam say.

"I love you," said Grant.

"I love you too," said Sam.

And with that, Sam's spirit vaporized and he was gone.

1999

Grantsville, Indiana

Epilogue

The nurse on the maternity floor at Grantsville Community Hospital wheeled in the cart with the Goldstein's newborn son. She smiled as she saw the delight on the faces of the new parents. From her conversations with Mary Goldstein during her eighteen hours of labor, she had learned that the thirty-five year old social worker and her husband had been trying for seven years to have a baby. They had seen infertility doctors, had lots of tests, and procedures. With no success whatsoever. Finally, they had given up, and were looking to adopt, when one day Mary realized that she hadn't had her monthly cycle in at least three months. A home pregnancy test had told her she was pregnant.

Mary had called her husband Ben, an accountant, at work, ecstatic, and he had advised caution until they could get the news confirmed by a doctor. The couple had waited anxiously for the day it took to get the lab results back.

When they found out they were indeed pregnant, they had felt that they were the two luckiest people on earth, that God had specially blessed them as he had Abraham and Sarah in the Bible, when Sarah had given birth at an advanced age, although Mary knew that thirty-five was not nearly as old as Sarah had been. Nonetheless, in keeping with Jewish tradition, they had bought nothing for the baby until after he or she was born.

Last night, after the baby had been born, Ben had gone home, where he and his brother had assembled the baby's crib. Mary's and Ben's mothers had gone together to purchase a layette for the baby, who they had named Herbert, in honor of Ben's late uncle.

The nurse handed the baby wrapped in his little hospital blanket to his eager mother, along with a tiny bottle of the formula the doctor had recommended.

Ben gazed at his son with wonder. The nurse excused herself, for she had several other newborns to bring to their parents for feeding time.

"His eyes look so familiar," Ben said to his wife.

The baby gazed directly at his father.

"He has beautiful eyes," said his proud mother. "Such a pretty shade of blue. Maybe they remind you of your uncle Herb, since he had blue eyes, too."

"No," said Ben, shaking his head. "I've seen those eyes somewhere, in a photo in a book somewhere."

Mary smiled, knowing that Ben would think about this over and over until he figured it out. Ben was a history buff, and he had hundreds of books at home in the large library room in their home. Ben was especially fond of the Civil War, Mary noted. "You'll figure it out," she smiled. "Would you like to hold him?"

She gave little Herb a gentle hug, and kissed one of his tiny little hands, then handed him to her husband.

"Hi, there, little guy," said Ben. "Welcome home to Mommy and Daddy."

The End

About the Author

Victoria Sauers is an author and historian who spends much of her time researching and writing historical fiction. She also works part-time as an exhibit preparator at a local museum, where the chair mentioned in this book is on display. She is the daughter of noted Civil War historian Dr. Richard Sauers and his wife Ayn. Ms. Sauers resides in western Pennsylvania.